Calm the Soul

A Book of Simple Wisdom and Prayer

The illustrations in the book come from The Poor Clares, Galway an enclosed order of contemplative nuns based in the heart of the city. The illustration used throughout is of the monastery in Nuns' Island, Galway, and others feature: San Damiano, Assisi, the first monastery of The Order of St Clare; Bethlehem, Athlone, the original monastery of the Galway Poor Clares; and Galway Cathedral.

Calm the Soul

A Book of Simple Wisdom and Prayer

The Poor Clares, Galway

HACHETTE
BOOKS
IRELAND

First published in Ireland in 2012 by Hachette Books Ireland
A Hachette UK company

This edition published in 2023 by Hachette Books Ireland

1

Copyright © The Poor Clares, Galway

A CIP catalogue record for this title is available from the British Library.

ISBN 978 1399 729192

Typeset in Centabel Book and Carolingia by Bookends Publishing Services, Dublin
Printed and bound in Great Britain by Clays Ltd, Elcograf S.p.A.

Hachette Books Ireland policy is to use papers that are natural, renewable and recyclable products and made from wood grown in sustainable forests. The logging and manufacturing processes are expected to conform to the environmental regulations of the country of origin.

Hachette Books Ireland
8 Castlecourt Centre, Castleknock, Dublin 15
www.hachette.ie

A division of Hachette UK
338 Euston Road, London NW1 3BH

Contents

Calm the Soul

When my boat, Lord, is storm tossed and sinking,
When fears in my heart take control,
Say 'Be not afraid' to my spirit,
And Your answer will calm the soul.

When I flounder around in deep waters,
When the stresses of life take their toll,
A sudden deep hush steals upon me,
Your gentleness calms the soul.

When my life seems too full of confusion
And I have lost sight of the goal,
As I stumble about in the darkness
May Your gentle light calm the soul.

I often live life on the surface,
Sometimes I'm playing a role,
Help me cherish my own inner beauty,
May Your tender love calm the soul.

When sinfulness tugs like an anchor,
When guilt has me caught in a hole.
I turn to You Lord for forgiveness,
And Your mercy calms the soul.

When I struggle with sickness and sorrow,
And eagerly long to be whole,
I call on Your name to bring healing
And the touch of Your hand calms the soul.

A Note on this Tenth Anniversary Edition

In the ten years that have passed since *Calm the Soul* was first published, much has changed in the world, yet the same perennial questions about the meaning of life and our role in the universe constantly stir within our hearts. As we find ourselves now in a post-pandemic world, one that is ever-changing and in which we are exposed to upsetting news stories on a regular basis, these questions have become all the more urgent. And in the midst of all of it, answers are difficult to find, and we can often feel insignificant and despairing. So where are we to find hope? We believe that our hope lies in encountering God's love for us.

As Pope Francis said in his opening speech on a recent World Youth Day, 'Can we truly believe that, unlike social-media algorithms that associate a name with "likes" and preferences, God truly knows our uniqueness, that His heart beats uniquely for us?' The values we encounter in the digital world of social media are often, though not always, a challenge to the

Christian understanding of our inherent dignity and value as children of God. Our worth lies not in how we look, in what we own, what we know, or who we think we are. It lies in our relationship with a God who loves us beyond belief – who died for love of us – and who calls us to a destiny beyond our wildest imaginings, to know and experience ourselves in our deepest essence to be eternally truly loved. Overexposure to the digital world can undermine this truth that we are of ourselves truly lovable.

Our intention with this updated edition of *Calm the Soul* is the same as the original: namely, to support those who wish to nourish or indeed reconnect with their relationship with God through prayer. This relationship enhances our humanity and equips us with the confidence and conviction that we have something to offer our fellow human beings and that we can help to make the world a better place. In this updated edition, we have included some new material, keeping in mind intentions that we are regularly asked to pray for. These intentions include prayers on anxiety, bullying, getting older and on using the Internet and social media.

It is important to remember that seeking medical and professional help may be necessary at particular times in our lives and be part of God's plan for us. While this is not a self-help book, we hope that its contents can show how a relationship with God – which is what prayer is – can help us to cope with life and relate

to the Lord in the ordinary reality of our daily lives and so encounter His healing grace and love. As you peruse the pages of this book may you experience the peace and joy of knowing and believing that you are a beloved child of God. Know too that you are in our prayers.

The Poor Clare Sisters, Galway

Introduction

Another book on prayer? It seems that there are so many as it is – why bring out another? Well, circumstances change and time stands still for no one. There have been phenomenal changes in recent times and we now live in a very different world, an extremely busy world. The reality is that, today, people are trying to juggle more and more activities in their day-to-day lives – earning a living, looking after children and homes, and studying, to name but a few. Advances in technology and the way we communicate have brought with them incessant demands for our attention.

We seek serenity of heart, but find that there is no space given for our souls. Silence is all but gone and, yet, silence itself can be healing. Allied to this is the reality that for many people, the pace of life has increased greatly. A rushed quality pervades our world and can rob us of peace. Living constantly on a treadmill, it is hard to appreciate how much our energy can be depleted through continued rushing. The result is that there is a high level of unease.

God wants us to live at peace, to have serenity and harmony in our hearts, but, today, these things can be difficult to find. Sometimes the importance of the spiritual aspect of life is not appreciated, and from what people have told us, by post or when they

visit the monastery, there's a real hunger for some tranquillity and silence. Despite the great changes that have occurred in our world, human nature is still the same, with the same needs.

The prayers and reflections in this book began on our website as a way to present ideas about prayer to people with busy, changing lives. St John Paul II asked Christian communities to become 'schools of prayer'. In this book we have brought together the fruits of our own prayer life to offer simple ideas on prayer in straight-forward, bite-sized portions.

As St Clare was the first female follower of St Francis, this book is permeated with a Franciscan flavour. The primary concern at prayer for both St Clare and St Francis, as in all of life, was the 'Spirit of the Lord and His holy activity'. This was the guiding force in their lives and if you were to ask them about prayer methods, they would probably recommend that you follow the lead of the Holy Spirit rather than force yourself into any particular method of prayer. The Holy Spirit leads each one of us in a different manner. That is the freedom and beauty of Franciscan prayer and is the essence we draw upon in this book.

Everyone is different and there is no such thing as the perfect way to pray. The important thing is to be open to the Holy Spirit and to allow yourself to be led in prayer. Because we are all individuals, each of the ways

of prayer in this book can be applied in different ways and will speak to each individual soul in a unique way.

When Jesus said, *'You must come away to some lonely place all by yourselves and rest for a while'* (Mark 6:31), it was an invitation to give ourselves a chance to have our batteries recharged and be refreshed by His grace. Our hope is that the simple ideas, prayers and reflections we have collated here will help to calm the souls of those who read them and will help each of you as you respond to the deep hunger for God which is written into every human heart.

St Clare

A Woman for Our Times

Clare Offreduccio, whom we know as St Clare of Assisi, may seem like a remote medieval figure. What could such a woman, who lived most of her life locked up in a monastery in Assisi in the thirteenth century, have to say to those of us living in this age of social media and artificial intelligence? What relevance could her life have for people living in the twenty-first century?

St Clare was the first female follower of St Francis of Assisi, and she has lived in his shadow for many years. However, she was no shrinking violet locked up in an ivory tower and unaware of the realities of life. As someone who had to fight to achieve what she felt was necessary, she has much to say to us.

Living at a time when women had little or no say in the way their lives were shaped, she emerged as a woman who lived her life in a resolute and passionate way, and who let nothing stop her from living out her vision of life as it began to unfold before her. She came under the influence of St Francis, having often heard him preach, and she met with him many times. This had to be done in secret because she was from a noble family, and they would certainly not have approved of her associating with such a strange man. But she could not

keep away because, in the words of her contemporary biographer, St Francis' words *'seemed to her, afire with God'* and it became clear to her that she was being called to embark on a new way of living with the Lord.

Leaving aside all security, she secretly left home on the night of Palm Sunday 1212 to join St Francis and his followers. It is hard for us today to imagine how shocking this must have been – a young, beautiful girl of eighteen going off on her own with a band of ragamuffin friars. However, she was single-minded and passionately in love with the Lord, and would not let anything stand in her way. When she later counselled in her letter to St Agnes of Prague that we should *'totally love Him who gave Himself totally for us'* (3 LAg 15), she was clearly speaking from experience.

Life was difficult in those early years. Originally, there was no specific monastery for St Clare to stay in but, eventually, she moved into San Damiano, one of the old churches that St Francis had repaired. Not long after she left home, she was joined by her younger sister Agnes and, eventually, many other women joined her (even her mother) – and so the Poor Clares began.

As leader of this group of women, St Clare had to be firm in her resolve to secure permission to live a radically poor way of life. In those days, it was unheard of for

monasteries of women to live without land or revenue to support them. However, St Clare wanted to embrace the Poor Crucified Christ in a radical way, and so she appealed to the pope in order to secure the *'privilege of poverty'* (a commitment to non-ownership in contrast to other religious orders at the time). Although highly thought of by three popes, each was very reluctant out of concern for the well-being and security of the sisters to grant this privilege to her. However, St Clare's conviction about poverty was crucial to her vision of life. Someone who lives in poverty is dependent on God and gives a clear testimony to her trust in Him.

She was also the first woman in Church history to write a rule of life for religious women and to get it approved. This was also something very close to her heart, as several different religious rules had been proposed for her community, none of which reflected the Franciscan ideal that she wanted to live. So, she set about writing her own 'Form of Life', which was approved by Pope Innocent IV the day before she died as she lay on her deathbed. Two years later, in 1255, her name was enrolled among the saints.

Such then was St Clare of Assisi – a woman of passion, courage and determination, with an all-consuming love for the Lord. Yet she was very gentle and considerate in her nature, something that is borne out by the

testimonies of her sisters and also her rule, which is noted for these traits. Down through the years, the noble and austere way of life she founded has never ceased to inspire and attract women who have the generosity and love to follow it.

Preparing
for Prayer

Why Pray?

Prayer is the food of the soul. Just as our bodies need nourishment so, too, do our souls which, in hungering for God, need to be nourished by prayer. Much of the stress that many people experience today comes from the fact that they neglect to nourish their souls. Our bodies, minds and souls make up a unit. Our society is becoming more and more geared towards looking after the body and the mind, but unless some harmony is restored by including the soul and bringing these three elements together, it is inevitable that people will experience anxiety. St Augustine said, *'You have made us for Yourself and our hearts are restless until they rest in You.'* A lot of the anxiety that people experience in their busy lives could be alleviated if some time was given to prayer and the search for God. Jesus is the Source of Peace and we cannot hope to have peace within ourselves unless we draw life from that source.

Essentially, prayer is a conversation with God, speaking to Him who created and loves us and listening to what He has to say to us. In this book, we want to offer a few different methods of prayer that we feel are well suited to the type of lives we live today. Prayer is a

relationship, so we all experience it differently. We have given examples of different types of prayer and hope that you will find an approach that suits you. Why not decide to spend ten or fifteen minutes a day in prayer? If you already do this, why not increase it to thirty minutes?

Prayer and holiness is for everyone in every situation. It is having our whole being in harmony with God's plan for us. We will never achieve true happiness if we continue to search for it outside the very source of love, which we know is God Himself. Scripture tells us that *'God is love'* (1 John 4:16).

As St John Paul II said in his letter on the dawn of the new millennium, why not *'start afresh from Christ'*? You won't regret it!

ꜰow τo Pray

Jesus tells us that, when you pray, you should *'go to your private room and, when you have shut your door, pray to your Father who is in that secret place, and your Father who sees all that is done in secret will reward you'* (Matthew 6:6). It is important that when we come to pray we give the Lord 'quality time'. Our prayer is a relationship, so we need to work on it.

> *One does not pray only when one has the time.*
> *One makes time for the Lord.*
> CCC 2710

We are human and prone to distractions, so we should avail of whatever supports to prayer are available. Try creating a suitable atmosphere, a quiet room, perhaps with candles and soft music. It is not necessary to have a set place for prayer, but it can be helpful. Sometimes, you may be able to visit a chapel. This has the added advantage that if the Blessed Sacrament is there, you are actually in the sacramental presence of the Lord Jesus. You should always begin with a prayer to the Holy Spirit, to help you to be open to His inspirations. Scripture says, *'The Spirit too comes to help us in our*

weakness. For when we cannot choose words in order to pray properly, the Spirit Himself expresses our plea in a way that could never be put into words' (Romans 8:26).

We could ask for His help in our own words or use a simple invocation such as *'Come, Holy Spirit'.* We can also use this beautiful prayer by Cardinal Mercier.

O Holy Spirit, soul of my soul
I adore you.
Enlighten me, guide me,
Strengthen me and console me.
Tell me what I ought to do
And command me to do it
I promise to be submissive in everything
That you ask me to do
And to accept everything that you permit
To happen to me.
Only show me what is your will
And give me the grace to do it.
Amen.

When we begin to pray, it is important that we become conscious that God is love and He loves us passionately. All our prayer is a response to the God who loved us first. God's love for us is a free gift, it is gratuitous. We don't have to earn this love. He loves you as you are

right now. As you come to pray, listen to Him speaking words of love in Scripture and realise that they are addressed to you personally. As you hear God speak, allow the reality of His love for you to penetrate your heart. *'I have loved you with an everlasting love. I still maintain my faithful love for you'* (Jeremiah 31:3).

There is a story from our Franciscan tradition that one night St Francis went through the forest, weeping because *'Love is not loved'*. He was deeply aware that God is Love and he found it heartbreaking that so many people ignored God. He lived his life as a response to that love. St Clare's response was *'totally love Him who gave Himself totally for your love'*. Our journey, too, is to reciprocate that love.

Always remember
God has called you into being
God loves you more than
you can ever imagine
God has a vital purpose for your life.

Silence

There is a real need for us to learn to appreciate the value of silence. The widespread use of technology impinges on us, maybe more than we realise. There always seems to be some level of noise. Though we may not fully be aware of how much it is affecting us, it has an impact. Even subtle 'white noise' in the background has an effect. While it may seem innocuous enough, we often feel drained by it, and it seems as if we can't hear ourselves think. Our senses can become overwhelmed. Noise contributes to us having difficulty sleeping, as our minds try to process everything with which we have been bombarded during the day. And then we wonder why our nerves are frayed and we are frazzled at the end of the day!

Silence is little respected today and yet it is essential for a healthy life and for prayer. Silence has so many benefits. It is like a blanket we wrap around ourselves to enable us to sink deeper into the true reality of life and into our being. When the very atmosphere possesses a profound peace and tranquillity, it lends itself to a gentler approach to living. It gives us a better capacity to listen both to others and to God. It helps to drain

away stress and tension and can bring with it a sense of calmness. We all know that silence is very important for meditation – vital in fact; the word of God penetrates more deeply when we have both outward and inward silence.

In music, we need both notes and rests – sound and the silence unite to produce a harmonious blend. This is a perfect analogy for our lives. Speech is good, but we also need to give time to open up these spaces of quiet in order to bring about harmony in our lives.

Silence can be challenging. While it is beneficial, it can also be painful, because it provides a space for the things that we have buried to surface. If this happens, the silence can also provide a forum in which we can bring these issues to the Lord and ask Him to heal us. We often live disconnected from our inner selves because we may have suppressed things that we do not like about ourselves. We need to let these things surface, and allow them to be healed and integrated. As each memory is awakened, we simply try to hand it over to the Lord for healing, for we read, *'Unload all your worries on to Him, for He is looking after you'* (1 Peter 5:7). See the recommendations in the 'On Healing' section in the Further Reading and Reflections chapter.

When we enter an undisturbed silence, we can be more attentive to the truth of who we are. It also provides an ambiance in which the Word of God can be received and cherished. While silence of itself is not prayer, it helps create an atmosphere conducive to prayer. To allow the Word of God to work on us, we need to let it penetrate our souls. We must allow our souls to become tranquil. Then, like drops of water sinking into a still pond, we let the ripples go forth, gently touching the deepest recesses of our hearts. Let the sound of these words of the Lord echo and re-echo within you and find a home there.

Ways to Pray

Intercession
and Petition

We are usually fairly good at the 'asking' type of prayer – it comes naturally to us when things go wrong or we are out of our depth. God is our loving Father who is anxious to provide for us and loves when we turn to Him in prayer. Intercession is possibly our most instinctive way of praying, and Scripture invites us to pray this way when Jesus says, *'Ask and you shall receive'* (Matthew 7:7). However, God also wants us to come to know Him and the fullness of His love for us.

We are told many things about this type of prayer. For example, *'If you find your delight in the Lord, He will grant you your heart's desire'* (Psalm 36/37:4). This is very similar to what Jesus tells us: *'Set your hearts on his kingdom first, and on his righteousness, and all these other things will be given you as well'* (Matthew 6:33). This means that when we come to intercede, we should look to the Lord and His righteousness first, to delight in His company and then to ask for what we need. It means that we do not take God for granted – and this makes sense, when we remember that the Lord wants us to enter into relationship with Him.

The way that Jesus interceded is an example for us. We often find that before He performed a miracle, He blessed God first. For example, before He raised Lazarus from the dead, He turned in thanksgiving to the Father (John 11:41–42). We also find Him blessing the bread before the multiplication of the loaves (Luke 9:15–16).

The 'Our Father' is a perfect example of this type of prayer. Here, the first three petitions are devoted to praise of the Father and praying for His will – only then do we move on to intercession as such.

Scripture also tells us, *'If two of you on earth agree to ask anything at all, it will be granted to you by my Father in heaven'* (Matthew 18:19). There is incredible power in unity of hearts at prayer, because God is the source of all unity.

One of the incidents from the life of St Clare that illustrates her style of intercession profoundly was when the sisters' monastery (which lay just outside the city of Assisi) was threatened by Saracen troops. Not only were they in mortal danger but so, too, was the city as the soldiers were on the way to attack it. St Clare was bed-ridden, but the sisters came to her in crisis. She asked them to bring her to the door of the monastery and then asked for the pyx, containing the Blessed Sacrament, to be brought out too.

Though she was sick, St Clare prostrated herself before the Lord in prayer, an act of profound worship. Then, holding the Blessed Sacrament aloft, she begged Him to defend her sisters, whom she could not defend. A voice, like that of a little child, was heard and it said, *'I will always defend you.'* Clare continued to pray, saying, *'My Lord, please protect this city which for Your love sustains us.'* The troops turned back and the city and the monastery were saved. This incident, perhaps more than any other, shows St Clare's great devotion to, and trust in, the Eucharist. It is why she is usually depicted with the Blessed Sacrament in a monstrance.

Praying in the
Spirit of St Clare

St Clare fell passionately in love with Christ. She had a distinct relationship with each person of the Holy Trinity – Father, Son and Holy Spirit – however, she focused her eyes and her affections on Christ, whom she said had become for us 'the Way'. With this love, she was able to face the trials that came her way. She was courageous and determined. She grew in understanding and became a very balanced person, which can be seen clearly in her writing. For both St Clare and St Francis, everyone was a brother or sister: all were treated the same. Everyone and everything was a gift, and their lives and spirituality were characterised by gratitude.

St Clare wrote no treatises on prayer. However, her letters to St Agnes of Prague form the central part of her writings and give us a marvellous insight into what animated her heart. St Agnes was a princess from Bohemia who had been much sought after in marriage, even by Emperor Frederick II. However, Christ had captured her heart and she resolved to give herself completely to Him. When she heard of the way of life

that St Clare and her sisters were following, she was attracted to what they were doing. She established a Poor Clare convent in Prague and began a correspondence with St Clare. Four of the letters survive and they are very important for helping us to appreciate St Clare's vision of life.

The letters provide a window into the soul of St Clare. They are less formal than the rule and in them we can see the progression in both St Clare's spirituality, as her prayer life matured and developed, and her deepening friendship with St Agnes. The letters show her as a very affectionate woman, capable of deep friendship and not afraid to express her affection openly. They also reveal her clarity of vision and her ability to home in on the essentials of life and living. These she articulated in a way that inspired St Agnes and those who have followed her down through the centuries. Their value is incalculable.

In the letters, you can detect the concern of a mother for her spiritual daughter, that she learn to know the Lord in an intimate manner. St Clare shares with St Agnes in a very natural way, giving her guidance from the depths of her own relationship with God. Using inspiring words and images, she hints at ways through which St Agnes could open her heart to enter into contemplation.

As a way to open up to a dialogue with the Lord, she has this to say:

> *Place your mind before the mirror of eternity!*
> *Place your soul in the brilliance of glory!*
> *Place your heart in the figure*
> *of the divine substance*
> *and through contemplation*
> *transform your entire being*
> *into the image*
> *of the Godhead Itself.*
> 3 LAg 12–13

'Place your mind before the mirror of eternity': The mind is the source of all our anxieties and fears. St Clare tells us elsewhere that Christ is the mirror, so to place our mind in the mirror of eternity is to bring all that we carry within us – our burdens and our joys – to the Lord. We come before the Lord as we are and bring them to Him. Reflecting on these things in the light of eternity has the advantage of helping us gain perspective on them. Often, our worries can diminish when we think of them in terms of eternity

In her fourth letter to St Agnes, St Clare said, *'Gaze upon that mirror each day ... and continually study your face in it.'* This is another starting point for our prayer – to come before the mirror, who is Christ, and

ask Him, 'What are You saying to me today? What do You ask of me?' Spend some time trying to listen for His response.

'Place your soul in the brilliance of glory': The soul is our innermost being, the meeting place with God. In each of us, there is a special hidden place where God waits for us. It is in the deepest caverns of our being, where God's Word can resonate within and be amplified, if we attune ourselves to His Presence. Although not a physical place, it is where God's Spirit resides within us. In this stage, we try to imagine entering into this sacred place. We ask the Holy Spirit to illuminate it with His light. We come here in reverence, knowing it is a sacred space. We try to come in stillness and silence, so that we can be attuned to the presence of God. We may not feel anything – that is all right. The important thing is to seek to encounter Jesus.

'Place your heart in the figure of the divine substance': Let transformation take place through contemplation. Christ is the figure of the divine substance. At this stage, we seek to involve our heart. We endeavour to rest in Him, trusting in His deep love for us. We can do this by expressing sentiments of love, if we feel comfortable with that. Scripture can help us greatly here and we can use a simple phrase, such as *'I have loved you with an everlasting love, so I am constant in*

my affection for you' (Jeremiah 31) or *'Do not be afraid, for I have redeemed you … you are mine'* (Isaiah 43). The essential point here is to do this gently. We allow ourselves to be docile in His hands, so that He can imprint Himself upon our souls.

Our aim in all of this is that, as St Clare said, we may *'feel what His friends feel'* and may *'taste the hidden sweetness'* of God. In this is true freedom of heart and where our souls may find ultimate peace.

Adoration with St Clare

Apart from Mass, the adoration of the Most Blessed Sacrament is one of the highest forms of prayer, centred as it is on Christ in the gift of Himself to us. Because He is God, He is worthy of all praise and adoration. Adoration is, above all else, an act of worship because we believe that Jesus is truly present. We look at Him with eyes of love, are moved with gratitude and we want to give Him the highest honour.

This practice of adoration is a beautiful way to prolong our encounter with Him in the celebration of Mass. When we come to adoration, we meet Jesus. It is He who has drawn us to this encounter and He longs for us to know how much He loves us. We place ourselves close to His heart, like the Beloved Disciple (John 13:25). We come to Him as we are.

There are many ways to pray at adoration – and many of the ways given in this chapter are suitable. It is good to use the time to deepen our relationship with Him – allow Him to get to know us and let Him reveal Himself to us.

St Clare is often portrayed with the Blessed Sacrament and is known for her devotion to it. Her advice was:

Gaze,
Consider,
Contemplate,
Desiring to imitate your spouse.
2 LAg 20

Breaking this down, we can see a beautiful way to pray.

Gaze upon Him: St John Mary Vianney, known as The Curé of Ars, who lived in the nineteenth century, spoke of a man who, when asked how he prayed, said, *'I look at Him and He looks at me.'* It is not so much a physical looking at Jesus, as putting ourselves in the presence of the One who loves us totally. We make ourselves present to Him and allow Him to look at our innermost being with His loving, healing gaze, letting the reality of His love change and heal us.

Consider Him: Having become aware of Jesus, we reflect on the reality of who He really is, as revealed to us in Scripture. Jesus came into the world to enter into our humanity fully. No matter what way we feel, there is something in Jesus' life that each of us can relate to. For instance, if we feel fearful, we recall Jesus' fear in Gethsemane, when He prayed, *'My Father, if it is possible, let this cup pass me by'* (Matthew 26:39). If we are burdened, we hear His invitation, *'Come to me, all you who labour and are overburdened, and I will*

give you rest' (Matthew 11:28–29). If we are worried about the future, we can bear in mind Jesus' words, *'I am telling you not to worry about your life and what you are to eat, nor about your body and how you are to clothe it. Look at the birds in the sky. Are you not worth much more than they are?'* (Matthew 6:25–26) Seeing afresh how Jesus works in people's lives, we can talk with Him about our life situation, and so form a relationship with Him.

For other quotations, see the 'Scripture for Reflection' section in the Further Reading and Reflections chapter.

Contemplate Him: Having spoken to the Lord about what is bothering us, we hand our cares over to Him, remembering the words of St Peter, *'Unload all your worries on to Him, since he is looking after you'* (1 Peter 5:7).

Then we rest gratefully in His loving presence, confident that He will take care of us.

As you desire to imitate Him: A fitting conclusion to a time spent in adoration with the Lord is to try to become more like Him. It is good for us to make some resolution at the end of our prayer time, even something small, like to smile more, so that we enter into solidarity with Jesus.

Prayer

*Jesus, send Your Spirit into my heart as
I come to You in prayer.
Give me the inner vision that St Clare had,
in order to see You as You really are.
Help me to become aware of Your
Presence with me,
especially in this time of prayer,
so that I may totally love You
who gave Yourself totally for love of me.
Amen.*

Praying with Scripture

Praying with Scripture is an enriching way to pray, to calm the soul. This is because using Scripture is like having a dialogue between yourself and Jesus (who is the Word of God). It contains so many comforting words from the Lord and these are like a balm to the soul.

Taking time with Scripture works on our souls in a deep way, even if we are not aware of it. Jesus compares the Word to a seed that is planted (Mark 4:26–39, Luke 8:11). We cannot see the growth and development under the soil – it is hidden, but it is happening nevertheless.

At the beginning, it can be difficult to know where to start with Scripture. It is a good idea to start off with the gospels (where we encounter Jesus) or the Psalms (which cover the entire gamut of human emotions and which can help us to process all that is going on within us). Take a phrase from the Bible and simply ponder over it. It is good to do this each day, so that the Word becomes part of our lives. Repeating the words embeds them in our minds and hearts.

Both St Francis and St Clare had such reverence for the Word of God that they said the way of life of their brothers and sisters was to live the Holy Gospel. As we come to a deeper appreciation of the Word of God, we may be drawn to give more time to this practice and want to approach Scripture in a more structured way. *Lectio divina*, a method of praying with Scripture from the monastic tradition, helps us to do this.

Lectio Divina

This consists of four stages – *lectio, meditatio, oratio* and *contemplatio* – and is much more than a reading or study of Scripture. It is an encounter in faith and love with the Word of God. If you can devote twenty minutes or so a day to this, you will find it very helpful. And, as you reflect on these texts, do not feel that you have to exhaust one text in one day. You can come back to the texts again and again.

Lectio (reading): Choose a passage of scripture and read the text a few times. If possible, read it aloud, as there is an additional dynamic in reading it aloud. This is because the texts were meant to be proclaimed, so while you might feel self-conscious doing this, it is helpful. Several of the senses are involved (sight, speech and hearing) and it will resonate within you. This is very important in *lectio* – to allow the Word to echo and re-echo and reverberate within you. Read lingeringly, with attention and love. This is not about getting through as much text as possible, it is about allowing the Spirit who inspired the text to work on your soul, so that you may know what He wants to say to you. Savour the words, and particularly stay with words which 'speak' to you.

Meditatio (meditation): At this stage, mull over the text and try to see where it is being fulfilled in your life today. Your memory and imagination will enter into action as you remember past events where you have seen the Lord working or, with your imagination, enter fully into the text and become part of what is happening. Meditation takes time, but it need not stop when you finish your prayer time as you can reflect on where this is being mirrored in your life at other times – as you wait for a train, are standing in line at the shops or as you mow the lawn. Try to come to an interior understanding of what is written. Take as your example Our Lady, who *'pondered'* in her heart the things that had been revealed to her (Luke 2:19, 2:51).

Oratio (prayer): This is where we respond to the Lord's promptings to us in the previous stages. Taking our cue from the words of the text (usually), we base our prayer response on what has happened to us as we pondered His Word. Pray from the heart, and the Holy Spirit will put into words what we may not be able to (Romans 8:26). Even if we feel that nothing has happened, in faith make some prayer response, because the Lord is constantly working within us and His Word is dynamic.

Contemplatio (contemplation): Contemplation is the beginning and end of *lectio divina*. This is about entering a deeper phase in prayer. It goes beyond what our senses can experience. It is a prolonged gaze of love. From this, we are called to go forth in active love of God and our neighbour.

When you begin to pray with Scripture, it is helpful to invest in a good version of the Bible, preferably with a commentary. Throughout this book we have used the Jerusalem Bible. It is helpful to read the Bible in context, and consulting a commentary can help us to do that.

Serenity and Surrender

Being fearful and anxious can cripple us, often leaving us paralysed. Fear begins with a thought, which often latches on to other fears within us, and takes hold of us, taking us captive. The more it gets a grip, the more we can be paralysed by it. To have courage is to feel fear, but to go beyond it. One of the things that is said in Scripture most often is, *'Do not be afraid.'* When St John Paul II addressed the United Nations in New York in 1979, he said:

> *... men and women must learn to conquer fear. We must learn not to be afraid, we must rediscover a spirit of hope and a spirit of trust. Hope is not empty optimism springing from a naïve confidence that the future will necessarily be better than the past. Hope and trust are the premise of responsible activity and are nurtured in that inner sanctuary of conscience where 'one is alone with God' and thus perceives that he or she is not alone amid the enigmas of existence, for they are surrounded by the love of the Creator.*

One of the most popular prayers of our time is the 'Serenity Prayer', capturing, as it does so well, that we often struggle to deal with things that are beyond us in our daily lives.

God grant me the serenity to accept
the things I cannot change;
The courage to change the things I can;
And the wisdom to know the difference.

Reinhold Niebuhr

If we can change things that need to be dealt with, we must seek to do this with God's help. However, the pathway to serenity is to realise that we need to turn to a Higher Power when things are beyond us. We need to learn to surrender to God and let His power work in the situation.

Fr Walter Ciszek, an American Jesuit, recounted his experiences of being captured by the Russian secret police during the Second World War. He spent the duration of the war in Lubyanka Prison in Moscow, mostly in solitary confinement. After this, he was sent to a labour camp in Siberia for fifteen years. He was eventually exchanged for two Russian spies and returned to America, only to discover that he had been officially listed as dead for sixteen years.

During his time in Lubyanka, he underwent many interrogations because the Soviets were convinced that he was a Vatican spy. One of his greatest trials was that, having endured daily interrogations for one full year, he signed a confession that his captors had prepared. He had reached the end of his strength. Then, he was left in solitary confinement, where he was haunted by what he had done, brought down with guilt and shame. Slowly, painfully, as he struggled with the darkness that enveloped him, he realised that he had been trying all along to do everything under his own steam. He was a physically fit man, having lived a disciplined life, and possessed a sharp intellect. Each day, he had gone into the interrogations determined to outwit the men and not to give in. In fact, having struggled for so long, he reached the point of despair.

In that moment, he threw himself before the Lord and accepted his helplessness. He cried out to the Lord when he recognised, as he says himself, that his own abilities were bankrupt and God was his only hope. He was consoled in that moment by recalling the Lord in the agony in the garden, where Jesus cried out three times, *'My Father, if it be possible, let this cup pass me by'* (Matthew 26:39). He appreciated that Jesus knew the feeling of fear and weakness in His human nature and yet He abandoned himself to the will of the Father each time.

At that moment, Fr Ciszek knew exactly what he had
to do. He realised that he had to surrender himself
completely to the Father and trust in Him to act in the
situation, instead of trying to control it himself. He
grasped that it was too big for him and that he needed
power from on high. It was only when he reached the
stage of being totally overwhelmed by everything that
he surrendered. In doing so, he crossed a boundary that
he had feared and yet, by doing this, he experienced
total liberation and a release from all his fears of the
future. He knew that he did not know what the future
held, but he was able to trust in God to sustain him.
He said:

> I can only tell you frankly that my life was changed
> from that moment on. If my moment of despair
> had been a moment of total blackness, then
> this was an experience of blinding light. I knew
> immediately what I must do, what I would do,
> and somehow I knew that I could do it.

And this resolution carried him for what remained of
his ordeal. He served another four years in Lubyanka,
followed by fifteen years in Siberia. This spirituality of
surrender sustained him through it all, being able to
live 'one day at a time' in the same way as those who
struggle with addictions.

Fr Ciszek's life is a clear witness for our times of the reality that serenity of heart comes through surrender to God. To pray in this way, to surrender, means to realise that we are helpless without God's help. We need to invite Him into the situation and hand it over to Him.

In this spirit, we offer a prayer of surrender adapted from the spiritual teachings of Fr Walter J. Ciszek SJ:

*Lord, Jesus Christ, I ask the grace to accept
the sadness in my heart, as Your will for me,
in this moment. I offer it up, in union with Your
sufferings, for those who are in deepest need of
Your redeeming grace. I surrender myself to
Your Father's will and I ask You to help me
to move on to the next task that You have set for me.
Spirit of Christ, help me to enter into a
deeper union with You.
Lead me away from dwelling on the hurt I feel:
to thoughts of charity for those who need my love,
to thoughts of compassion for those
who need my care,
and to thoughts of giving to those who need my help.
As I give myself to You, help me to provide for the
salvation of those who come to me in need.
May I find my healing in this giving.
May I always accept God's will.
May I find my true self by living for*

others in a spirit of sacrifice and suffering.
May I die more fully to myself, and live
more fully in You.
As I seek to surrender to the Father's will,
may I come to trust that He will do everything for me.

To surrender to God is to let ourselves be open to His action in our lives. Reaching out to others can help broaden our perspective which, in turn, can help diminish our own pain. It is important to remember that this giving can be as simple as the gift of a smile.

Forgiveness

And when you stand in prayer, forgive whatever you have against anybody, so that your Father in heaven may forgive your failings too. But if you do not forgive, your Father in heaven will not forgive your failings either.
Mark 11:26

No book on prayer would be complete without looking at forgiveness as prayer and a way to pray. It is an absolute prerequisite. The above quotation, beginning with, *'When you stand in prayer ...'*, reveals that real prayer can only flow from a heart willing to forgive. Forgiveness must be at the beginning of prayer.

The reason for this is that an absence of forgiveness is like an acid that burns away at us, eating into our very being. We feel hurt by someone, and part of us wants the person who caused the hurt to feel pain for what we perceive they have 'done' to us. However, when we dwell on it, we find ourselves replaying the situation over and over again in our heads, rehearsing what we wish we had said or done, or what we will say or do at the next opportunity! Unfortunately, we can

get sucked into this; sometimes it almost takes on a life of its own and it draws us deeper and deeper into itself. In the end, we cause ourselves more suffering. This is why Jesus stresses the need for forgiveness over and over again. If we don't forgive, we actually end up hurting ourselves. Each time we replay what has happened, we feel the pain again and it gets worse – it's like picking the scab off a wound; it bleeds again and can fester.

So, what is the solution?

We can't do it on our own. We require the grace of God to forgive, but we also need to co-operate with Him in this. God asks us to bless our enemies, and when we try, His grace comes to help us. Paradoxically, when we try to see the good in others, especially those who have hurt us, when we try to understand them, it diminishes the toxic quality of our anger and we start to feel calmer. As we continue to do this, we can begin to feel peace returning to our souls. It does not change the past, but it can change how we see the past and how the future will be.

It is important to realise that forgiveness is not a matter of feelings, but of the will. If we focus on our wounds, we are staying with ourselves and not focusing on God. We may not feel like forgiving someone and we may

not feel as if we like them. We are not called to 'like' people, but to love them. And so we make a decision to forgive and to let go of the injury. If necessary, we surrender it to God, so that He may take over. In its essence, forgiveness is a gift we give to ourselves.

Forgiveness has another effect too. The prayer we make on behalf of those who have hurt us also has an effect on them. We may not perceive this straight away, but it is true nonetheless. Slowly, and sometimes imperceptibly, their hearts receive healing too.

The following suggestion from Fr Silvester O'Flynn is helpful:

> *If you are finding it impossible to forgive somebody, it shows that you have not yet discovered the Holy Spirit within you, the Spirit given to you in Baptism. Your natural love is focusing towards that person whom you can't love. Supernatural love thinks less of towards and more of from, the source of divine love within us. Hand over this problem of forgiving to God-within-you. Confess to God that your natural ability has reached its limits. Invite God-within-you to think in your mind and to love through your heart.*

All of the this will help with the day-to-day hurts that we all experience. However, sometimes an acute hurt may need deeper healing to reach the root of the pain. We may need to seek further help. The Lord often uses other people to minister to us. We may need counselling or to ask someone to pray for or with us. The suggestions given above are not a substitute for counselling when this is needed, they are given to help deal constructively with the issues that come our way each day.

The Sacrament of Reconciliation or Confession is the great source of healing and peace in difficult situations. It is a sacrament instituted by Jesus and He underscores its importance in the gospels. While it may seem very daunting to have to confess your sins to someone else, especially if you have not been to Confession in a long time, it is truly liberating, because our faith teaches us that, through the priest, it is the Lord Jesus Himself who absolves us from our sins. There is no greater freedom and joy than that experienced when you hear the words, *'I absolve you from your sins … The Lord has freed you from your sins. Go in peace.'* And this is the reality – the burden of those past sins has been taken from us and we can come to know inner peace.

As Jesus said the evening before He died, this peace is *'a peace the world cannot give'* (John 14:27).

Nevertheless, sometimes life may put us in situations that are completely unjust. We can experience hurt and we cannot understand why – there is no way to make sense of the situation, because it does not make sense. At these times, a heroic level of forgiveness may be asked of us. We need to keep our eyes and hearts firmly on Jesus and realise that this is exactly what He went through. Never was such a grave injustice done to anyone as happened to Him, and yet His prayer was: *'Father, forgive them: they do not know what they are doing'* (Luke 23:34).

While this is a difficult prayer to say when a grave injustice is being done, it goes to the depths of what our faith is about. Even if people are intentionally hurting us, they may not fully know what they are doing. To pray *'Father forgive them for they know not what they do'* is to enter into the mystery of redemption with Jesus and to trust that, in the end, His love and sacrifice will win out.

Contemplation

Contemplation is difficult to write about. As it is a wordless form of prayer, how do we find words to describe it? It is a concept-less form of prayer, so how do we find the concepts to explain it?

We are in the realm of mystery – God's mysterious way of communicating with the soul. It is because of its very intimacy that it goes beyond words. As with an embrace, words are not necessary, but very deep communication is happening nevertheless. As we are on holy ground, we have to remove the sandals from our feet (Exodus 3:5) leaving behind our finite ideas which seek to contain God within our own understanding.

And yet, we should bear in mind that while contemplation is beyond concepts, it is not something that happens in a vacuum, nor are we trying to empty our minds. For St Clare and St Francis, their prayer, as with their whole lives, was centred on the person of Christ. St Clare put it beautifully when she wrote, *'totally love Him who gave Himself totally for your love'.*

Contemplation is beyond concepts because Jesus Christ is not a concept, but a person, a divine person. We seek an encounter with the One who loves us. It is a relationship that we are cultivating here, not mindlessness. Therefore, in this type of prayer, we try to put ourselves in His Presence and rest there. The prophet Hosea expressed it well when he said, *'I am going to lure her and lead her out into the wilderness and speak to her heart'* (Hosea 2:16). Blessed John Henry Newman put it more succinctly: *'Heart speaks to heart.'*

At the very heart of contemplation, we allow God to work out a transformation within us. As St Clare wrote to St Agnes of Prague:

> *Place your mind before the mirror of eternity!*
> *Place your soul in the brilliance of glory!*
> *Place your heart in the figure of*
> *the divine substance*
> *and through contemplation*
> *transform your entire being into the image*
> *of the Godhead Itself.*

St Clare captures very well what this type of prayer is about. She speaks about contemplation as bringing about the transformation of our entire being into God Himself. The words she uses make it seem as if we do this work of transformation. In fact, she is well aware that only God can accomplish this within us.

That is why she says *'through contemplation'* because contemplation is God's work within us. Earlier in the quotation, she asked St Agnes to 'place' herself three times before the Lord – place her mind, place her soul and place her heart. It is only in our surrendering of these faculties to God that He can carry out this work. When this happens, we can co-operate with God so that this transformation can take place.

The goal of contemplation for St Clare is to allow ourselves to be open to the work of God, so that we may *'feel what His friends feel'* and *'taste the hidden sweetness'* of God.

When we start to practise this type of prayer, we find that we have all sorts of distractions. We are so used to being busy, that our minds are constantly processing things. When we try to quieten down, suddenly all the things we have to do come to mind. The really important thing is not to worry too much about this – just let those thoughts go and, as St Clare says, *'place your mind'* again before the Lord. He knows the way we operate and He just wants us to keep gently handing over everything to Him. If we imagine our prayer as a river, then these 'thoughts' are merely bits of things floating along – that's just the way it is. We don't want to grab on to them, we just see them and let them go.

It may seem strange to propose this to people with busy lives. It is true that it can take time to cultivate

this type of prayer, because it is based on developing a relationship with Christ. Obviously, it is more effective if we give quality time to this. However, once you have started, it is possible to 'check in' at any time. It is like making a quick call or sending a text – it says I am still here and want to connect. The first friars had no fixed houses and so couldn't talk about 'houses of prayer', so St Francis, who was often on the move, drew on the tradition of the early monasteries and talked about entering the 'cell' of his heart. For St Francis, every friar was in himself a 'house of prayer'. He said, *'The body is our cell; and the soul is the hermit that lives in the cell in order to pray to God and to meditate'* (*Mirror of Perfection*, 65). When he was travelling, he used to wrap his cloak about him in order to pray. For us, there are often moments when we can simply close our eyes and lift our hearts up to the Lord.

It is important to stress that this type of prayer is not about feelings. The action of God operates at a level that is deeper than the senses. We may have pleasant feelings or we may not – it doesn't matter, because this prayer is about love, real love. It requires us to be faithful. Love is a decision. We make a commitment and then take what comes. We need to be careful not to try to measure our 'success' and we should certainly never evaluate our prayer by our feelings. When you are down, don't give up.

Commitment

So far, we have reflected on the significance of prayer for our lives. It is vitally important for serenity in our souls that the way we pray is mirrored in the reality of what is happening in our lives. If these things are out of sync, then we begin to lack authenticity and may find it leads to disharmony within. Our lives should be a sign of what we believe interiorly. St Clare urges us to praise God by our very lives (3 LAg 41) and so genuine prayer, which requires commitment, spills over into our lives.

Looking at how St Clare gently led her friend St Agnes, we see that the main way to have our prayer in harmony with our life is to be clearly focused on the Lord and to try to stay committed to whatever we begin. There is a general fear of commitment today, but it is very true that in being dedicated, we grow and mature. St Clare herself kept before her eyes the *'one thing necessary'* (Luke 10:42), as Jesus said to Martha, and she can even say, *'I bear witness to that one thing and encourage you, for love of Him to whom you have offered yourself as a holy and pleasing sacrifice, that you always be mindful of your commitment'* (2 LAg 10).

What follows is so beautiful, we let St Clare speak to us herself:

What you hold, may you hold.
What you do, may you do and not stop.
But with swift pace, light step, unswerving feet,
so that even your steps stir up no dust,
may you go forward
securely, joyfully and swiftly,
on the path of prudent happiness,
believing nothing,
agreeing with nothing
that would dissuade you from this commitment
or would put a stumbling block for you on the
 way,
so nothing prevents you from offering
your vows to the Most High in the perfection
to which the Spirit of the Lord has called you.
2 LAg 1 1 –14

Prayer

*St Clare, we ask for the grace, through your
intercession,
of being focused and single-minded.
Help us to remember how much God loves us.
May we be true to the commitments we have made
and not be afraid.
May we have courage, when this is needed,
and go forward in hope as you said,
'securely, joyfully and swiftly',
on the path of prudent happiness,
so that we may glorify God by our lives.
Amen.*

Everyday
Prayers

We offer here a more traditional selection of prayers. Given our busy day-to-day lives, we are not suggesting that you take on all of them, just choose one or two that appeal to you. You could use them in the morning and evening, to begin and end the day with the Lord.

Act of Faith

You believe because you can see me.
Happy are those who have not seen and yet
believe.
John 20:29

Faith is vital in prayer. When Jesus performed miracles, He invariably said, *'Your faith has saved you!'* This is somewhat surprising. You might think that He would have been more impressed by people's love or their other virtues, but, no, it was faith that He responded to. In fact, when He visited Nazareth, we are told that He was unable to perform many miracles there because there was so little faith in that town. So it seems He was prevented by people's lack of faith. Perhaps this is because, when we demonstrate faith, it shows that we trust God and this removes any barriers that may be in our hearts. As St Mark tells us, *'Everything is possible for anyone who has faith'* (9:23).

An 'Act of Faith' is not so much a prayer for faith, as an assertion of our belief. In saying this prayer, we give due honour to God and also put our faith into practice. This very exercise helps to deepen and strengthen our faith.

Act of Faith

My God,
I believe in You and in
all Your Church teaches,
because You have said it
and Your Word is true.

Act of Hope

The 'Act of Hope' articulates that our hope is fuelled by our belief. We believe the promises of Christ, because He is God and speaks the truth. Hope is also strengthened by confidence in His infinite power.

Perhaps it is nourished most of all by our trust in God's mercy. Mercy loves when love is not deserved. If we were to get what we truly deserve, we would have no hope. But we need have no fear of Him or the future.

It might seem that faith and love are more important. But actually it is hope that bolsters up our faith and our love. In the nineteenth century, Charles Péguy wrote a poem in which there were three sisters who had joined hands – Faith and Love are the big sisters with the little girl, Hope, in the middle. Looking on, it seemed that Faith and Love were helping the little girl but, as they got nearer, it was Hope, running ahead, who brought her sisters along. Hope reminds us that we are reaching towards a greater goal than the more immediate ones. It urges us to keep going.

Our 'Act of Hope' is not so much a prayer for hope, as an articulation of the hope we already have, trusting that in exercising this hope, it will grow.

Act of Hope

My God
I hope in You for grace
and glory,
because of Your promises, Your mercy
and Your power.

Act of Love

*Nothing therefore can come between us and the
love of Christ, even if we are troubled or worried,
or being persecuted, or lacking food or clothes,
or being threatened or even attacked.*
Romans 8:35

Jesus said the greatest commandment was to love *'the
Lord Your God with all your heart'* (Mark 12:29). He
continued, *'You must love your neighbour as yourself'*
(Mark 12:31). However, love is not about how we feel.
We make the decision to love and then carry through
with it. We may feel that we don't love God with all
our heart. Still, we must aspire to it and keep the ideal
before our eyes, to inspire us to keep trying. God
deserves our best.

Our 'Act of Love' reinforces these sentiments in our
hearts and helps to strengthen our resolve to love.
Clearly, we cannot do this without God's grace.

From the depths of your heart love God.
St Clare

Act of Love

My God,
because You are so good,
I love You with my whole heart,
and for Your sake,
I love my neighbour as myself.

Act of Contrition

Give me again the joy of Your help,
With a spirit of fervour sustain me.
Psalm 50

One of Jesus' most popular stories is the parable of
the Prodigal Son (Luke 15). It reveals the true picture
of the Heavenly Father, who watches out for His
children, running out to meet them. We also see His
young son, rehearsing his lines – *'Father, I have sinned*
against heaven and against you. I no longer deserve to
be called your son.' However, the father, who is slow
to anger and rich in mercy, does not let him finish his
speech, but runs out to embrace him and reinstates him
with his dignity as his son. Similarly, we often reject the
loving advances God makes towards us, even in spite
of ourselves.

In Psalm 50, which is said to have been composed
by King David after he had committed adultery and
murder, we see how liberating repentance is. King
David realised the enormity of what he had done
and turned to the Lord, trusting that he would not be
rejected.

In praying our 'Act of Contrition', we repent of the hurt caused by our betrayals, both of God and of our brothers and sisters. We ask for His grace, so that we may be strengthened interiorly and be energised to make a new beginning, a fresh start.

Act of Contrition

My God, I am very sorry
I have sinned against You,
because You are so good,
and with the help of
Your grace I will not
sin again.

Our Father

The 'Our Father', or 'The Lord's Prayer', as it is also known, holds pride of place among all other prayers. It is what Jesus taught the disciples when they said to Him, *'Lord, teach us to pray'* (Luke 11:1). Therefore, it is a precious gift from our Saviour to us and we should treasure it as such.

A good way to pray the 'Our Father' is to imagine Jesus is standing beside you, perhaps holding your hand, or with His arm around you. The fact that the prayer starts off with 'Our Father' and not 'My Father' is an indication that we are not alone when we pray this prayer.

It is through what Jesus accomplished for us that we have been adopted as children of the Father and, in this prayer, we can go to the Father, accompanied by Jesus. If we fully realised what a privilege this is, to call God (the Creator of the universe) our 'father', we would spend our whole lives giving thanks for it. In fact, when St Francis used to pray the 'Our Father', he was so overwhelmed by this fact that he often got no further than the words 'Our Father' and stayed with those words in love and adoration.

Our Father

Our Father who art in heaven,
hallowed be Thy Name.
Thy kingdom come.
Thy will be done on earth, as it is in heaven.
Give us this day our daily bread,
and forgive us our trespasses,
as we forgive those who trespass against us,
and lead us not into temptation,
but deliver us from evil.

The Chaplet of Divine Mercy

This devotion focuses on the great merciful love of Jesus for us, which caused Him to suffer and die for us. It revolves around trust in the Lord and appealing to Him for mercy. It has many wonderful promises attached to it. In addition, the repetition of the simple invocations has a soothing effect, especially on those who are dying.

Regarding the chaplet, Our Lord said to St Faustina:

Encourage souls to say the Chaplet which I have given you ...

Whoever will recite it, will receive great mercy at the hour of death ...

When they say this chaplet in the presence of the dying,

I will stand between My Father and the dying person, not as the just Judge but as the Merciful Saviour ...

Priests will recommend it to sinners as their last hope of salvation.

Even if there were a sinner most hardened, if he were to recite this chaplet only once, he would receive grace from My infinite mercy ...

I desire to grant unimaginable graces to those souls who trust in My mercy ...

Through the Chaplet you will obtain everything,
if what you ask for is compatible with My will.

How to Pray the Chaplet of Divine Mercy

To pray the Chaplet, you may use a Rosary beads. Begin with one 'Our Father', one 'Hail Mary' and the 'Apostles' Creed'. (See 'Prayers of the Rosary', page 84, for the 'Apostles' Creed'). Then, on the 'Our Father' bead, pray the following:

> *Eternal Father, I offer you the Body and Blood, Soul and Divinity of Your dearly beloved Son, Our Lord Jesus Christ, in atonement for our sins and those of the whole world.*

On the ten 'Hail Mary' beads, pray the following:

> *For the sake of His sorrowful Passion, have mercy on us and on the whole world.*

Repeat for five decades.

To conclude the chaplet, say:

> *Holy God, Holy Mighty One, Holy Immortal One, have mercy on us and on the whole world. (three times)*

The Holy Name of Jesus

St Francis set an example of a tender devotion to the Holy Name of Jesus. In his biography, it is recounted that when he pronounced or heard the name 'Jesus', he was filled with joy *interiorly and seemed to be altered exteriorly as if some honey-sweet flavour had transformed his taste, or some harmonious sound had transformed his hearing'*. For St Francis, pronouncing the Name of Jesus was a means of entering into a loving communion with the Son of God. It can be the same for us.

In fact, pronouncing the Holy Name of Jesus with love and trust is the shortest of prayers. In a busy world such as our own we can find ourselves in difficult situations unexpectedly. The Name of Jesus, spoken with love and reverence, can then be a source of comfort and support when all else fails. For those struggling with suicidal thoughts or addictions it is a particularly powerful help when temptations are strong.

Jesus is our friend and helper on life's journey. He cares about our every need and loves us unfailingly and constantly. Calling on His Name makes Him present to us in a very real way. He wants to effect in our lives

what His Name means. He wants to save us. It is a particular blessing to have the Name of Jesus on our lips as we pass from this world to the next.

The prayer we offer here was composed to mark the centenary of the beginning of a new wave of devotion to the Holy Name of Jesus in Ireland which began in our monastery.

'I tell you most solemnly anything you ask for from the Father, He will grant in My name.'
John 16:23

Prayer to Invoke the Holy Name of Jesus

Jesus, Yours is the name above all names;
we offer you our heartfelt praise and gratitude.
Deepen in us an abiding reverence
for Your Holy Name.

Jesus, Saviour, heal the wounds within
that our sin and fear have inflicted.
Set us free from all that hinders us from
rejoicing in Your boundless love
and sharing Your goodness with others.

Jesus, Friend, draw us ever closer to You.
We entrust all we carry in our hearts
to Your abundant mercy.

Jesus, Lord, pour out
the Holy Spirit upon Your people
that our lives may overflow with Your grace,
our days be filled with Your love,
and all our actions shine with your light.
Amen.

Novena to the Sacred Heart

Many of us in years gone by will remember seeing a picture or statue of the Sacred Heart. It was usually given a prominent place in most Irish homes and was often accompanied by a little red lamp.

The origins of this devotion go back to the thirteenth century and our own St Bonaventure. In following the footsteps of St Francis, St Bonaventure desired to reveal to people the beauty of the Incarnation of Our Lord, and what better way than to speak of the love in the Heart of Jesus for each one of us.

Four centuries later, Our Lord appeared to St Margaret Mary Alacoque in France. When resting her head on His chest, she could hear His beating Heart. He asked her to spread this devotion and attached twelve promises to those who prayed to him under the title of the Sacred Heart of Jesus. June is the month of the Sacred Heart.

The most recognisable phrase associated with this devotion is: *'Sacred Heart of Jesus I place all my trust in you.'*

Novena to the Sacred Heart

You have said, O Divine Jesus,
'Ask and you shall receive, seek and you shall find,
knock and the door shall be opened unto you.'
Relying on these promises, I come with confidence
during this novena to beg of You the favours I need
(make your request here)
From whom shall I ask, Lord Jesus, if not from You,
whose Heart is an unfailing source of grace.
Most loving Heart of my God,
I believe in Your power,
I believe in Your knowledge,
I believe in Your personal love for me.
And therefore, O Sacred Heart of Jesus,
I place all my trust in You.

Praying to Our Lady

In her third letter, St Clare says, *'Cling to His Most Sweet Mother.'* For St Clare, Our Lady is always mentioned in relation to Jesus. He is always the focus of her attention but, being a woman deeply in love, she understands the depth of the love that exists between them – and, being the 'mother' of at least fifty sisters in her monastery, she knew what was involved in this role. A mother always has time for all her children and has all their interests at heart. She unifies the family, is a refuge when we are afraid, the one we can always turn to, no matter how much we think others may not love us or, indeed, how much we may not love ourselves! Jesus gave His mother to us as our mother in a special way on the Cross, and so St Clare knew that we can all approach Our Lady in complete confidence, knowing that we will not be turned away and that she will draw us ever closer to her Son.

When we pray to Our Lady, we seek to develop a relationship with her. We take time to talk to her and share our worries and joys with her. We confide in her, let her become a true mother to us. If we *'cling'* to her, as St Clare suggests, she won't let us down.

On Prayer to Our Lady

Look to the star – call upon Mary!
In danger, in difficulty or in doubt,
think of Mary, call upon Mary,
keep her name on your lips,
never let it pass out of your heart.
Following her footsteps,
you will not go astray;
praying to her,
you will not fall into despair;
thinking of her you will not err.
While she keeps hold of your hand,
you will not fall,
you will not grow weary,
you will have no fear.
Enjoying her protection,
you will reach the goal.
Mary, Star of the Sea, pray for us.
St Bernard

Hail Mary

Hail Mary,
Full of grace,
The Lord is with thee.
Blessed art thou amongst women
And blessed is the fruit of thy womb,
Jesus.
Holy Mary, mother of God,
Pray for us sinners now
And at the hour of our death.
Amen.

Memorare

Remember O most gracious virgin Mary,
that never was it known
that anyone who fled to your protection,
implored your help or sought your intercession
was left unaided.
Inspired with this confidence, I fly unto you,
O Virgin of virgins, my mother;
to you do I come, before you I stand,
sinful and sorrowful;
O Mother of the Word Incarnate,
despise not my petition,
but in your mercy hear and answer me.
Amen.

The Rosary

If the 'Our Father' is Jesus' gift to us, then most certainly the Rosary is Our Lady's gift to us, her children. In the Rosary, we meditate on the mysteries of the life of Jesus in the company of Mary. It is an entirely scriptural prayer, the simplicity of which is deceptive.

It is a form of prayer that is particularly suitable for people with busy lives. The rhythmic repetition of the prayers has a calming effect on us. The Rosary is at the service of opening our hearts to Jesus that He may dwell there and that we may come to know His love which surpasses all knowledge.

In a world where the value of silence is little appreciated, praying the Rosary together gives a 'window' of opportunity for silence, when the family is together. A family that tries to do this can carve out a quarter of an hour in the day where there is silence, which creates a deep bond in the Spirit, even without there being any awareness that this is happening. It may not seem that it actually is a silent time in the strict sense, but these moments spent praying with Our Lady subtly deepen the unity of the family.

How to Pray the Rosary

The Rosary is a meditative prayer on the mysteries of Christ's life. The complete Rosary consists of four sets of mysteries – the Joyful Mysteries, the Sorrowful Mysteries, the Mysteries of Light and the Glorious Mysteries – each prayed on different days of the week.

The Rosary begins with the Apostles' Creed prayed on the crucifix of the rosary beads. Then an 'Our Father', three 'Hail Marys' and a 'Glory be to the Father' are prayed on the beads which connect the crucifix to the circle of beads.

Then follow the mysteries of the Rosary. Each mystery is announced and may be followed by a short pause for reflection on that mystery.

The decade begins with one 'Our Father', ten 'Hail Marys' and one 'Glory be to the Father'. According to custom the 'Fatima Prayer' may then be said, and the next mystery is then announced and prayed in the same way and so on.

When the five mysteries are completed, one 'Our Father', one 'Hail Mary' and one 'Glory be to the Father' are added for the pope's intentions. Then the 'Hail, Holy Queen' prayer is said.

For more insights on the Rosary see the 'Reflections on the Rosary by St John Paul II' section in the Further Reading and Reflections chapter.

The Joyful Mysteries

Prayed on Monday and Saturday

The Annunciation
The Visitation
The Birth of Our Lord
The Presentation in the Temple
The Finding of the Child Jesus in the Temple

The Sorrowful Mysteries

Prayed on Tuesday and Friday

The Agony in the Garden
The Scourging at the Pillar
The Crowning with Thorns.
The Carrying of the Cross
The Crucifixion

The Mysteries of Light

Prayed on Thursday

The Baptism of Jesus
The Wedding Feast of Cana
The Proclamation of the Kingdom
The Transfiguration
The Institution of the Eucharist

The Glorious Mysteries

Prayed on Wednesday and Sunday

The Resurrection
The Ascension
The Descent of the Holy Spirit on
   the Apostles and Our Lady
The Assumption
The Crowning of Our Lady as the
   Queen of Heaven

The Prayers
of the Rosary

The Apostles' Creed
Fatima Prayer
Hail, Holy Queen

The Apostles' Creed

I believe in God,
the Father Almighty
Creator of heaven and earth.
And in Jesus Christ,
His only Son, Our Lord
Who was conceived by the Holy Spirit,
born of the Virgin Mary,
suffered under Pontius Pilate,
was crucified, died and was buried;
He descended into hell;
on the third day He rose again from the dead;
He ascended into heaven,
and is seated at the right hand
of God the Father Almighty;
from there He will come to judge
the living and the dead.
I believe in the Holy Spirit,
the holy Catholic Church,
the communion of saints,
the forgiveness of sins,
the resurrection of the body,
and life everlasting.
Amen.

Fatima Prayer

O my Jesus, forgive us our sins,
save us from the fires of hell;
lead all souls to heaven,
especially those in most need of Your mercy.

Hail, Holy Queen

Hail, Holy Queen, Mother of Mercy; hail, our life, our sweetness and our hope! To you do we cry, poor banished children of Eve; to you do we send up our sighs, mourning and weeping in this valley of tears. Turn then, most gracious advocate, your eyes of mercy towards us; and after this our exile, show unto us the blessed fruit of your womb, Jesus. O clement, O loving, O sweet Virgin Mary.

V. Pray for us, O Holy Mother of God.
R. That we may be made worthy of the promises of Christ.

Let us pray.
O God, whose only-begotten Son, by His life, death and resurrection, has purchased for us the rewards of eternal life; grant we beseech you, that meditating on these Mysteries of the most holy rosary of the Blessed Virgin Mary, we may both imitate what they contain, and obtain what they promise, through the same Christ our Lord.

R. Amen.

The Angelus

This prayer is a wonderful way to bring our hearts and minds to the Lord during the day. It is traditional to pray it at 6 a.m., 12 noon and 6 p.m. – literally at morning, noon and night! It has the effect of sanctifying our day as we begin it (at daybreak), during the course of the day (by pausing to pray at midday) and by ending our day in thanksgiving at 6 p.m., which equates to sundown. 'The Angelus' focuses on the mystery of the Incarnation of the Lord and reaches its climax with the breathtaking proclamation of St John, *'The Word became flesh and dwelt among us.'*

When we pray this prayer, we pray that the implications of Jesus becoming one with us, in order to save us, may be fully realised in our lives. In 'The Angelus', Our Lady is held up to us as a model, for her prompt and whole-hearted response to the Lord, *'Let what you have said be done to me'* (Luke 1:38). We ask that her prayers may help us to respond as she did. We pray that the Lord will pour forth His grace into our hearts, so that by the power of His passion, we may be brought to the glory of His resurrection.

Praying 'The Angelus' is also an opportunity for us to be more 'bold' about our faith: stopping for this prayer is a simple but powerful witness to our belief.

The Angelus

V. *The Angel of the Lord declared unto Mary.*
R. *And she conceived of the Holy Spirit.*

The 'Hail Mary'

V. **Behold the handmaid of the Lord.**
R. *Be it done unto me according to Your Word.*

The 'Hail Mary'

V. *And the Word was made flesh.*
R. *And dwelt among us.*

The 'Hail Mary'

V. **Pray for us, O Holy Mother of God.**
R. *That we may be made worthy of the promises of Christ.*

Let us pray. Pour forth, we beseech You, O Lord, Your grace into our hearts, that we to whom the Incarnation of Christ, Your Son, was made known by the message of an angel, may by His passion and cross be brought to the glory of His resurrection, through the same Christ Our Lord. Amen.

May the divine assistance remain always with us and may the souls of the faithful departed, through the mercy of God, rest in peace. Amen.

Prayer to my
Guardian Angel

O Angel of God my guardian dear,
To whom God's love commits me here,
Ever this day (night) be at my side,
To light and guard, to rule and guide.
Amen.

Morning Offering

Almighty Lord God,
You have brought us to the beginning of another day.
Strengthen us with Your grace,
so that during this day we may not fall into any sin,
but may direct all our thoughts, words and actions,
to accomplish Your Holy Will.
Through Christ our Lord.
Amen.

Prayer at Night

Jesus, Mary and Joseph, I give you my
heart and my soul,
Jesus, Mary and Joseph, assist me now and
in my last agony,
Jesus, Mary and Joseph, may I breathe forth
my soul in peace with you.
Amen.

Into Your hands

Into Your hands
Lord, I commend my Spirit.
Lord Jesus, receive my soul.
Amen.

Daily Prayer
for Protection

Heavenly Father, in the name of Jesus,
I put my conscious mind, my unconscious mind
my subconscious mind, my thoughts, my memory
my emotions and my words
under the protection of the Precious Blood of Jesus.
Establish Your Lordship in me
and keep me as Your own.
Amen.

Prayer for the Whole Human Family

This prayer was written by St Augustine:

Keep watch, dear Lord, with those who work,
or watch, or weep this night,
and give Your angels charge over those who sleep.
Tend the sick, Lord Christ, give rest to the weary,
bless the dying, soothe the suffering,
pity the afflicted, shield the joyous,
and all for Your love's sake.
Amen.

Prayer Before the Crucifix

This prayer was written by St Francis:

Most High,
glorious God,
enlighten the darkness of my heart
and give me
true faith,
certain hope
and perfect charity,
sense and knowledge,
Lord,
that I may carry out
Your holy and true command.

Prayer for Peace

Though not written by him, this prayer is attributed to St Francis, as it reflects the dispositions of his heart.

Lord, make me an instrument of your peace,
Where there is hatred, let me sow love;
Where there is injury, pardon;
Where there is doubt, faith;
Where there is despair, hope;
Where there is darkness, light;
And where there is sadness, joy,
O Divine Master,
grant that I may not so much seek
to be consoled, as to console;
to be understood as to understand;
to be loved as to love.
For it is in giving that we receive;
It is in pardoning that we are pardoned;
and it is in dying that we are born to eternal life.

Prayer for the Faithful Departed

Eternal rest grant unto them, O Lord,
and let perpetual light shine upon them.
May they rest in peace.
Amen.

Praying to
the Saints

Devotion to the saints has always been an important aspect of the Catholic tradition. God is the origin of every good, the One from whom *'every good and perfect gift comes'* (James 1:17). Seeking the intercession of the saints does not imply that we doubt God's power or love or willingness to help us directly. We don't need the saints to 'put in a good word' for us with our loving God. The saints simply want to share the gifts of grace that they received on earth through the *'one mediator between God and humanity, the man Christ Jesus'* (1 Tim 2:5).

God bridged the gap between divinity and humanity in the Person of Jesus when the Second Person of the Blessed Trinity took on our human nature and became one of us, a phenomenon that we call the Incarnation. And it is through Him, the 'one Mediator between God and humanity' that we invoke the intercession of the saints as our heavenly friends who are rooting for us and care about us and who, in Christ, want to help us. All the 'power' of the saints flows from Christ. The Catechism of the Catholic Church (no. 956) puts it this way.

'Being more closely united to Christ ... [the saints] do not cease to intercede with the Father for us, as

they proffer the merits which they acquired on earth through the one mediator between God and men, Christ Jesus ... So by their fraternal concern is our weakness greatly helped.'

We can form attachments to different saints who may appeal to our individual personalities and it is good to form a relationship with a saint, to treat as a friend, a guide, showing us how to love. The saints have particular charisms or gifts, stemming from gifts they had on earth or crosses they had to bear in their lives. It means that they have a unique power of intercession in those areas and can be special intercessors (or patrons) for us when we have similar struggles. In fact, the Church often appoints a particular saint as a patron of a particular domain or activity. St Joseph is the patron saint of fathers and carpenters, St Clare the patron saint of television, St Martha is the patron saint of cooks, St Anthony is a reliable friend who will always find what you have lost, and there are many more examples.

We include in the following pages a little background on some of our favourite saints as well as prayers for their intercession regarding different special intentions.

Prayer to St Clare

For an introduction to praying with St Clare, see pages 22–30.

Blessed St Clare,
You trusted in the Blessed Sacrament
as your only protection.
In your hour of need you heard a
voice from the Sacred Host:
'I will always take care of you.'
We entrust our needs to you, especially
(here mention requests)
Help us to trust Him as you did.
Enkindle in us a tender love for Jesus and Mary.
Intercede for our families, our friends,
our youth and all those who need our prayers.
We pray for our church, our country
and our suffering world.
Amen.

Praying to St Joseph

St Joseph was chosen by God to be the spouse of Mary. In the scriptures, he is revealed as a strong yet gentle man. While he experienced inner turmoil on learning of Mary's pregnancy, he showed a readiness of will, like Mary's, with regard to what God asked of him through the Angel, who informed him of the origin of the unborn Child.

He was a man of tremendous courage and initiative, shown when he travelled to Egypt to protect the little baby Jesus from Herod's soldiers who slaughtered all babies around Bethlehem, thus ensuring that this child, the promised King of Israel, would be spared.

At Knock Shrine in County Mayo, Ireland, St Joseph appeared together with Our Lady and St John, the only time he is known to have appeared to anyone. He came as a tall, silent and protective figure, casting his gaze towards Our Lady and Jesus, who came as the Lamb of God. He reveals himself as truly humble, someone who is powerful with God – though how could he be otherwise: he was chosen by God to be the earthly father of His Son, Jesus.

His principal feast day is celebrated on 19 March but he is also honoured as patron saint of workers and that feast day is held on 1 May. St Joseph is also the patron saint of the universal church and the dying.

Prayer to St Joseph

O glorious St Joseph,
You who have power to render possible
things that are for us impossible,
come to our aid in our present
trouble and distress.
Take this important and difficult
affair under your particular
protection,
that it may end happily.
O dear St Joseph, all our confidence
is in you since you are so powerful
with Jesus and Mary.
Let it not be said that we would
invoke you in vain.
Amen.

Prayer to St Francis

Intercessor for those coping with the
burden of responsibility
Intercessor for the Environment

St Francis must be one of the best-known and loved saints, whose popularity and relevance endures to this day. Primarily associated with love for all creatures, whom he looked on as his brothers and sisters, and known as a man of peace, there are many more facets to him and his life.

He had many struggles in his life, such as illness, failure in battle, a difficult relationship with his father, as well as the hardship of living a life of poverty, and these prepared him for the work God had in mind for him. Because he is seen as a carefree person it is not often appreciated that he also had to deal with conflict in different situations and the worries that come with responsibility, especially as his Order of Franciscan brothers grew. This is clearly illustrated in a charming story told about St Francis in the *Fioretti di San Francesco (The Little Flowers of St Francis)*.

Once, before St Francis had any companions, he was invited to visit at the home of Bernard of Quintavalle, a wealthy nobleman, who wanted to see if the man who was generating so much interest in Assisi was genuine. After, they spent the evening in conversation, Bernard invited St Francis to stay, intending to watch what St Francis would do during the night. When bedtime came, they retired. Bernard pretended to be asleep and began snoring. After a while, St Francis arose and fell on his knees to pray. He spent the entire night in prayer, repeating over and over again, 'My God and my All'. Bernard observed him and was, according to the story, 'touched by the Holy Spirit and resolved to change his life'. The following day he told this to St Francis who rejoiced greatly, and they prayed together. Bernard then gave all his wealth to the poor and followed St Francis.

The author of the *Fioretti* tells us that while St Francis was praying that night, he was made aware of the plans the Lord had for his life and about the Order that would be formed. He felt overwhelmed, becoming fully aware of his weakness and his limitations. He knew he couldn't do all he had been asked to do by himself and would have to rely totally on God's power, and so he claimed this power, by saying to God, 'My God and my All'. It was this humble trust in God to provide for him that so attracted Bernard and

he thus became the first person to follow St Francis as a Franciscan. It brings to mind the words that God spoke to St Paul, *'My grace is enough for you. My great strength is revealed in weakness'* (2 Cor. 12:9).

Perhaps we can all relate to this feeling – seeing what lies ahead (insofar as we can see what lies ahead) and feeling swamped by the magnitude of the task. In situations like this, it is extremely helpful to pray in the way St Francis did, entrusting ourselves and our needs to God, acknowledging that He is all-powerful and that we need His help. God cannot resist us when we show that we trust Him. It is glorifying God, and at the same time, imploring His help as our 'All'.

Here we offer the Novena prayer to St Francis that we use in the days before his feast day on the 4 October:

Novena Prayer to St Francis

Holy St Francis,
help me to respond joyfully, as you did, to God's loving invitation to fulfil my baptismal calling.

Obtain for me that same faith, hope and love that enabled you to joyfully renounce the pleasures of earthly life and to radically follow our Lord Jesus Christ.

*May I willingly suffer with and for the poor and show
reverence for all of God's creation.*

*Help me to be always grateful for the blessings
that I have received. If it is God's will please
intercede for me that …
[mention your intentions here]*

*May the blessings obtained through your
intercession deepen our faith,
and inspire us to seek treasures in Heaven,
in communion with our Lord and Saviour, Jesus
Christ, Our Lady and all the saints.
Amen.*

St Francis is universally known and loved as a
person who lived in harmony with creation. He saw
all creatures as children of God, and 'he would call
creatures, no matter how small, by the name of
"brother" or "sister"' as his biographer and disciple St
Bonaventure said. St Francis's reverent stance before
the beauty and wonder of all God's creation continues
to influence the modern ecological movement.

In *Laudato Si*, his encyclical on care for our common
home, Pope Francis took inspiration from the *Canticle
of the Creatures*, in which St Francis praises all the
different elements of creation and calls on them to join

him in praising the Lord. He opens up the encyclical by saying *'St Francis of Assisi reminds us that our common home is like a sister with whom we share our life and a beautiful mother who opens her arms to embrace us.'* (LS 1). And Pope Francis notes that it is important for us to approach nature and the environment with an openness to awe and wonder – without this respectful attitude, we are more likely to look at the environment with the mindset of a consumer or an exploiter.

Deeply conscious of this and inspired by the example of St Francis, we invoke his intercession as we pray to our Father.

Prayer For the Protection of the Environment

Heavenly Father,
We thank You for the wonder of Your Creation.
In Your servant Francis we see one who
joyfully embraced all of creation.
He looked on all Your creatures as his
brothers and sisters and he invited them to join him
in praising You.

*We pray for his intercession now for our
planet which needs our help.*

*We pray for an ecological awakening in the
hearts of all to these urgent problems that we may live
in a way that respects nature and hold all
creatures in profound reverence as St Francis did.*

*We pray for all those whose lives have been
devastated because of the exploitation of
nature, that they will get the help they need to
rebuild their lives.*

*We pray that nations will work together to
heal the damage which has been done, so
that we can all look to the future with hope.*

*We ask this in Jesus' Name.
Amen.*

St Thérèse of Lisieux

Intercessor for special intentions

It is hard to overestimate the influence that St Thérèse has had on Catholic spirituality in the twentieth century and right up to our own day. She was born in 1873 and died of tuberculosis at the young age of twenty-four in 1897. In her lifetime, a time when spirituality was dominated by an emphasis on the justice of God as opposed to His love and mercy, she developed a spirituality which has come to be known as the 'Little Way'. It emphasised the mercy and compassion of God and in practice consisted of small humble acts of love and virtue unseen by anyone (rather than showy heroic deeds): smiling when she didn't feel like it, being patient with a cranky old nun, being kind to another who seriously tested her patience. She showed us that true greatness – we could say true holiness – is really something very ordinary and simple and lies in attention to seemingly minor details of everyday life carried out for the love of God and our neighbour. She makes the idea of living a spiritual, compassionate life 'doable' for everyone.

Thérèse described herself as a 'Little Flower of Jesus' because she saw herself as a simple wildflower which

goes unnoticed. Unlike a brilliant rose or an elegant lily, she was growing and giving glory to God by simply flourishing in her small, humble way. And she is now widely known as 'The Little Flower'. St Thérèse arrived at the conviction that her vocation was to be, as she said, 'love in the heart of the Church' and she famously said that after her death she would 'let fall a shower of roses' and that she would spend her 'heaven doing good upon earth'. Many people have received favours through her intercession and report receiving a rose as a sign that their prayers are heard. Because she has kept these promises she is one of the most popular saints in the history of the Church. With all this talk of flowers, it is no surprise then that St Thérèse is the patron saint of florists and flower growers!

Our oldest sister remembers that, shortly after she entered the convent, elderly nuns remarked to her that she was blessed to be 'growing up' in the era of the spirituality of St Thérèse. They would say to her, 'You were blessed because you had the Little Flower' with her emphasis on the approachability and mercy of God as opposed to the inaccurate image, from an older spirituality, of a harsh, demanding God of whom many of them were afraid.

In our community library, as might be expected, there are whole shelves of books dedicated to the lives and spirituality of St Clare and St Francis. St Thérèse is the

only other saint who takes up a full shelf! Though not a Poor Clare her simple spirituality is very much in tune with our Franciscan ethos. It is a remedy for the anxiety of the modern age which demands high levels of performance in so many areas, even in the area of prayer. St Thérèse, by her life, example and teaching, shows us that everything we have and are is a gift from God and that our call is to respond to that goodness and love by receiving God's gifts and sharing them with others in simple, sincere and humble ways.

Because she also held the role of assistant Novice Mistress in her community, St Thérèse is the patroness of our novitiate and has always been held in great esteem by our sisters over the decades since her death. Here we offer a popular short prayer asking St Thérèse's intercession:

Prayer to St Thérèse

*Little Saint Thérèse, remember your promise
to do good upon earth.
Shower down your roses on those who pray to you.
Obtain for us from God the graces we hope for from
His infinite goodness especially …
We ask this through Christ our Lord
Amen.*

St Faustina

Intercessor for those who struggle
to answer the call of God

St Faustina Kowalska was born in Poland in 1905, the third of ten children born into a poor farming family. She is known to the world as the 'Apostle of Divine Mercy' or the 'Secretary of Divine Mercy' because during the course of her life as a nun she received many messages directly from the Lord Jesus who wanted her to spread the message of the unfathomable Mercy of God that is available to all. These messages form part of her diary in which she recorded everything that was communicated to her in these revelations. *The Devotion to the Divine Mercy*, as it is known, derives from these heavenly communications and has brought and continues to bring spiritual solace and inner healing to millions of people, drawing many back even from the brink of despair. If St Faustina had ignored the call of God how much poorer our world would be.

However, her biographies sometimes pass over the fact that she had a major interior struggle before she got the grace to answer that call. Her parents were

diligent in bringing her up with faith, yet when she announced to them at the age of seventeen that she wished to follow the call to religious life – a call she first perceived at the age of seven – they flatly refused to give their permission. She describes in her diary what happened next:

> After this refusal I turned myself over to the vain things of life, paying no attention to the call of grace although my soul found no satisfaction in any of these things. The incessant call of grace caused me much anguish; I tried however to stifle it with amusements. Interiorly I shunned God, turning with all my heart to creatures. However God's grace won out in my soul.
> (Diary Notebook I, 7–10)

Sometime later St Faustina attended a dance with her sister but while everyone else was having a good time, she found herself in deep torment about ignoring her calling. Suddenly she had a vision in her soul of the Lord Jesus, covered with wounds as at His Passion. He asked her: *"How long will you keep putting Me off?"* When the vision disappeared, she pretended to her sister that she had a headache and slipped out of the dance to go to the nearby Cathedral. There, she threw herself before the Blessed Sacrament, begging the Lord to give her understanding about what to do next. Then she heard the words: *'Go at once to Warsaw; you will enter a convent there.'*

And that's what she did, becoming a nun at the age of twenty, receiving the religious name Sr Maria Faustina. From that time on, she responded generously to God's call to such a degree that she rose to a great height of holiness and was canonised on 20 April 2000, the first saint of the new millennium. Although her spiritual journey was somewhat extraordinary – it is rare to hear the voice of God directly when we are trying to discover His will for our lives – the essential struggle that she experienced is the same for anyone who sincerely wants to do God's will, whether this is the call to religious life, or some other type of call. She shows us that it is okay to struggle with this and that God will give us the grace that we need to respond with generosity, finding peace and joy in trusting God completely as she did.

Heavenly Father,
I feel a stirring in my soul when I hear or read
about those who have joined religious orders.

I feel I am made for more.

I know that the experiences I'm having in my
life right now, in my work and in my relationships
are all good in themselves. Yet why then do I
feel this restlessness in my soul?

Sometimes I fear that I may have a vocation to religious life. This terrifies me. When I think of all the changes and sacrifices that I would have to make and all the people (especially those I love) that I would upset if I answered the call, I want to run the other way.

Now that I have come to know Your love for me, the thought of not answering Your call is as painful to me as any sadness I might cause to others. I want what You want for this life of mine which is Your gift to me.

Through the intercession of St Faustina, who intimately knew the struggle that I am experiencing, help me to know Your will and plan for my life and give me the grace and courage I need to follow it.

I also ask that You place wise guides in my path who will help to clarify Your plan for my life, and I entrust my family and those I love to Your Divine Mercy.

I ask all of this in Jesus' Name.
Amen.

St Thomas More

Intercessor for those wishing to live a life of integrity
Intercessor for courage in the face of opposition

Born in 1478, St Thomas More was an English lawyer, politician and statesman renowned for his honesty, literary prowess – he was the author of the socio-political satire *Utopia* – and his dedication to religious practice. He refused to recognise the annulment of Henry VIII's marriage to Catherine of Aragon and his subsequent marriage to Anne Boleyn. He also refused to acknowledge Henry as the supreme head of the Church of England. For this he was charged and convicted of treason. When it became likely that he was going to be executed, St Thomas More wrote an affectionate letter to his daughter Margaret *(Divine Office, Volume III, 62)*, while imprisoned in the Tower of London, in which he demonstrated an unshakeable trust in God and total surrender to God's will:

Mine own good daughter, never trouble thy mind, for anything that ever shall keep me in this world. Nothing can come but that which God wills. And I make myself very sure that whatever that be, seem it never so bad in sight, it shall indeed best.

He was beheaded on 6 July 1535 and famously said 'I die the King's good servant, but God's servant first'.

St Thomas More's deep spirituality shows that holiness is possible for people in all walks of life. He is the patron saint of diplomats and politicians. His outstanding integrity, even in the face of death, has made him a person that truly inspires us.

We begin our prayer of Intercession with four lines written by St Thomas More himself while imprisoned in the Tower of London. We first came across these lines on the Golden Jubilee card of a priest-friend of our community.

Thank you, dear Jesus,
for all you have given me,
for all you have taken away from me,
for all you have left me.

Through the intercession of your
faithful servant St Thomas More
give me patience in suffering the trials of life
in whatever form they come to me

I especially ask the courage to give faithful
witness to You and to the values of the Gospel

when they are unwelcome
and when I am unpopular on their account.
Let not bitterness, harshness or unforgiveness
gain a foothold in my heart

Help me now in this present situation ...
[insert details here]
Jesus I trust in You.
Amen.

St Elizabeth of Portugal

Intercessor for reconciling those in conflict

St Elizabeth of Portugal (also known as Isabel) was born into the royal family of Aragon in 1291. She was the grandniece of St Elizabeth of Hungary who is Patroness of the Secular Franciscan Order, founded by St Francis for those who are not called to religious life.

She was given in marriage to Denis, king of Portugal, at a young age, to forge a political alliance. Unfortunately, her husband was volatile and unfaithful, but she dedicated herself to a life of prayer, devotion and charity. She also devoted herself to seeking peace with her husband – eventually this was achieved, and he left behind his old ways to share a life of devotion with her. Her reputation as a peacemaker was further solidified when she managed to bring about healing in her husband's relationships with his brother, his son and his son-in-law in the midst of a vicious war. Following her husband's death, she became a member of the Secular Franciscan Order.

Years later, when her son marched his troops against her grandson, she rode onto the battlefield, at sixty-five years of age, and the two enemies were shamed into a genuine reconciliation. She died as a result of this last peace-making initiative in 1336.

While her greatest attribute was her gift of reconciling enemies, people also found her to be a woman with a clear mind, a strong character and a heroic trust in God born of a deep prayer life. She was canonised in 1625.

When we find ourselves in the midst of conflict and division, especially in our families, St Elizabeth is a good advocate. Having lived through several turbulent relationships, which threatened to tear her family apart, she never gave up hope.

Feel free to adapt the following prayer according to your circumstances.

Dear St Elizabeth,
As a wife and a mother you knew the heartache of seeing your family at loggerheads with each other even to the point of violence and hatred.

I ask you now to intercede for me in this difficult situation. I find myself in the crossfire between _____ and _____. I long with all my heart for them to reconcile so that we can be at peace again.

I know that nothing is impossible to God and I trust that you will intercede for me so that I can be an instrument of peace and reconciliation in this situation.
Amen.

Sᴛ Charbel Makhlouf

Intercessor for Miracles

St Charbel was born in Lebanon in 1828. He became a monk in the monastery of St Maron in Annaya, living a life of sacrifice and abstinence. He was granted permission to live as a hermit in the monastery of St Yaaqoub Al Hossom in 1875, and died there, on Christmas Eve 1898.

The remarkable sanctity of this saint only became apparent after his death. A few months after he died, his tomb began emanating light and this continued for forty-five days. His body was subsequently exhumed and found to be incorrupt, with none of the expected signs of decomposition visible. A number of attempts were made to hide his body because a strange liquid was exuding from it. His remains were eventually put in a standing position behind a glass door for veneration and it remained that way until he was reburied 1927. However, a strange reddish liquid continued to exude from his body wherever it was kept. His body was exhumed again in 1952 and his remains were still intact. When the grave was reopened again later the body

was completely decomposed and only his skeleton remained. To this day the reddish oily liquid continues to exude from the coffin.

St Charbel never had a picture of himself taken yet the images of him we have are based on a photograph taken in 1950 in which he miraculously appeared with other monks many years after his death. In 2016 an Australian woman suffering with cancer went to the Monastery of St Maron for a blessing but it was closed. She met a monk there who offered to bless her and she asked her son to take a photo of them. She subsequently shared the photo with a Lebanese friend who recognised St Charbel in the image. On returning to Australia she found she was healed of her illness.

Many miracles have been attributed to St Charbel – in fact upwards of thirty thousand recorded miracles have been linked to him.

He was canonised in 1977 and his reputation as a powerful intercessor has continued to grow. A popular shrine in honour of St Charbel has been erected in St Mary's Church in Headford, Co. Galway, to which many people travel seeking his intercession.

Prayer

O Merciful Father,
You chose St Charbel to be a worker of miracles.

He relished Your Divine Word which spoke clearly to
his heart as he prayed with the Scriptures.

In prayer he experienced your Presence especially
as he prayed before the Blessed Sacrament and
encountered Jesus there as the Bread of Life. He had
a particular love for Our Lady and experienced her
maternal love for him and all humanity.

We now ask you through his intercession to grant
our special requests …
[mention here your request]

We give praise to You through Your Only-Begotten
Son in the Holy Spirit forever and ever.
Amen.

Blessed Marie-Céline, Poor Clare

Intercessor for those in broken families
Intercessor for those living with disability

Jeanne-Germaine Castang was a remarkable young French woman who became a Poor Clare and died at the age of nineteen from tuberculosis, having lived through many traumatic events in her short life.

She was born in Dordogne in 1878, one of eleven children and initially theirs was a happy home. When she was four, Jeanne-Germaine contracted polio, which left her with a permanent limp. She did not let her disability keep her back from living as fully as possible and helping in the home, especially with the younger children.

Her father tried many businesses, but all were unsuccessful and he eventually led the family into financial ruin. Ultimately they had to leave their home and move into a damp, derelict barn in a very remote place where they lived for three years. They were so poor during that time that Jeanne-Germaine had to beg for food from the local farms, even though an

infection on her foot made this very difficult. Relations became strained within the family as they lived in this squalor.

Her father eventually found work in Bordeaux and the family moved there when Jeanne-Germaine was nine. However great damage had been done to their health in that barn, with some of the children dying from malnutrition and tuberculosis in the months that followed. Jeanne-Germaine was taken in by the Sisters of Nazareth who ran an orphanage and workhouse. She was happy with her work there but found it difficult being separated from her family.

When her mother died in 1892, Jeanne-Germaine came home for the funeral only to find her beloved elder brother very ill with tuberculosis. So she stayed to look after him and her two younger sisters. There was no bed for her, so she slept on the floor of her brother's room to tend to him during the night, which resulted in Jeanne-Germaine contracting tuberculosis herself. Sadly, her brother died shortly after her return home. By this stage, her father was a broken man and had to leave his job after his wife's death. So, the family had to be broken up: her younger sisters were taken in to be cared for by an Order of nuns which another sister had already entered and Jeanne-Germaine returned to the workhouse.

Her other older brothers had long since left home and had become estranged from their father.

Jeanne-Germaine was broken hearted after leaving them, as the memory of the family situation tore at her heart. She tried to comfort her father and sisters in her letters, and wrote to her brothers too, but in reality there was little contact in the family. Her father wandered around for a time, with no fixed abode, so she didn't even know if he received her letters.

She was deeply troubled by the enmity between her father and her brothers and got permission to take a trip to see them. She went to her father first. He did not receive her very well, but she was able to lavish him with care and soften him towards the idea of a reconciliation. She then visited one of her brothers and brought about a joyful reconciliation.

Having done this, she again started to consider her religious vocation. She had desired to consecrate her life to God in a religious Order from an early age but was turned down by every Order she applied to because of her illness. However, providence intervened when she and a friend visited a Poor Clare monastery in Talence, near Bordeaux. The Abbess recognised her vocation and Jeanne-Germaine was accepted to enter there in June 1896 at the age of eighteen. She received the

name 'Sr Marie-Celine of the Presentation'. Sadly, she soon became seriously ill with tuberculosis and died in the monastery on 30 May 1897 with a reputation for holiness. After her death she would make her presence felt through sweet fragrances which earned her the nickname 'Saint of the Perfumes'.

Her holiness was ratified by the Church when she was declared 'Blessed'. When a holy person is declared 'Blessed' or 'beatified' it means that the Church has investigated the person's life and established that they had heroic virtue. A further requirement is that a miracle through the person's intercession must occur and be attested to by doctors as having no medical explanation. In the case of Sr Marie Céline all these requirements were met and she was beatified on 16 September 2007.

Heavenly Father,
In your handmaid Blessed Marie-Celine,
You have given us a model of perseverance and
endurance in the face of huge obstacles.

She continued to reach out joyfully to help people
in need even as she battled with her own disability.
Though sensitive by nature, she seldom gave in to
feelings of self-pity, but focused on how she could
help others.

I ask her intercession for help in my own life, in the
times when I am struggling.

I pray also that she will intercede for healing in
my family and help me to be a force for unity and
reconciliation.

I bring before You now the other intentions of my
heart, especially … [insert details here]

We ask all this in the Name of Jesus Christ Your Son.
Amen.

Blessed Carlo Acutis

Intercessor for all young people

Blessed Carlo Acutis was a young Italian who died in 2006 at the age of fifteen of an aggressive form of leukaemia. Although not as yet canonised (the final phase of becoming an official saint of the Catholic Church), there is a growing devotion to him as an intercessor for young people. He himself had great devotion to St Francis of Assisi and loved visiting Assisi where his family had a second home. Carlo was highly gifted in computing and Internet technology, using his talents to educate people about faith and especially about the Eucharistic miracles which have occurred around the world over the centuries and in recent times.

Pope Francis has said of Carlo that through his gifts he communicated the values of the Gospel and that he was able to avoid getting sucked in by the mechanisms of consumerism and distraction which can prevent young people from offering the world those unique personal talents that God has given to each of them. One of Blessed Carlo's most famous quotations is: 'everyone is born as an original but many people end

up dying as photocopies'. Many young people today feel an intense pressure to be accepted by their peers and may sometimes act in such a way that they are not true to themselves and do or say things for the sake of being 'different' to impress those around them. Carlo however, had such a strong sense of his identity as a child of God that he didn't feel the need to be 'different' from everyone else. He was happy to be just himself. He is a model of how to be a young person in the twenty-first century deeply in tune with his faith in God while still being able to fully enjoy life with friends and family.

Here we offer a prayer for young people based on Blessed Carlo's thoughts and Pope Francis's exhortation to young people, *Christus Vivit* (2018), in which he drew on the life of Carlo Acutis as a model for young people to follow. Carlo showed by the way he lived his life that he knew, as the first lines of the exhortation says, that Jesus Christ is alive, that He is present in our lives at every moment and that He comes to us today and every day to give us life in abundance.

Heavenly Father,
I thank you for the gift of my youth. May I not waste it,
but rather may it be filled with purpose, meaning and
whole-hearted dedication to serving You and others.

Through the intercession of Blessed Carlo give me a
fresh outpouring of Your Holy Spirit so that my youth
may be a special time of grace, worthwhile in itself,
and not just a prelude to adulthood. When I feel weak
or disillusioned renew me in your love in your Son
Jesus. He is the one who is present in my life at every
moment, filling me with light especially at times when
I experience sorrow and loneliness.

Attentive to Your will for my life, may I steadily
pursue my hopes and dreams as Blessed Carlo did
with commitment, patience, and trust in You.

When I make mistakes, help me to see them as
opportunities to learn and to grow so that I may
become the person that You want me to be, not a
'photocopy' but a unique 'original' with a unique
contribution to make to the world.

I ask this in Jesus' Name.
Amen.

Venerable Matt Talbot,

Intercessor for those struggling with addictions

Matt Talbot may not be a household name and is little-known outside of Ireland, but he is an extraordinary intercessor for those who struggle with addictions of any kind. Knowing the life of addiction from the inside, he has become a 'wounded healer', whose prayers are very efficacious. Our community prays the prayer following this piece every evening for all those who are struggling with addictions. Many to whom we have recommended it feel that his intercession has helped them on the road to healing.

Matt Talbot lived in Dublin and died in relative obscurity there in 1925. He was the second of twelve children. His father and all his brothers, except his older brother John, were heavy drinkers.

Matt's first job, working for a company that bottled beer, began when he was twelve years old. He started to drink the dregs of the beer bottles, and by the age of fourteen, he was drinking whiskey. As his drinking worsened over the years, it became the sole focus of his life – he worked extra hours to feed his habit and borrowed money too. He also became a thief and many

years later he was plagued by regret for having stolen the fiddle of a blind man. He tried hard to locate this man to make this right but was never able to.

This addictive behaviour went on until Matt was twenty-eight years old. On a particular day in 1884, he had no money to buy himself a drink at the pub. As he had always been generous in treating others to a drink, he felt confident that there would be someone to treat him to one – but nobody offered. He was stunned. It was a wake-up call which brought home to him the futility of the life he was living. He resolved, there and then, to give up alcohol. He took the abstinence pledge and successfully abstained from alcohol for the rest of his life.

He struggled very much as he withdrew from his addiction and began to take long walks to avoid the pub or friends who might try to bring him there. On these walks, he began calling in to churches as a place to rest and avoid temptation but slowly turned to God for strength to stay sober, and rediscovered his faith. He began to live an intense life of prayer and penitential practices, rising at 5am each morning so he could attend early Mass before work. He began to live frugally but also gave generously to those who were struggling financially.

Matt died of a heart attack on 7 June 1925 at the age of sixty-nine. His fame as a holy man who had turned his

life around by the grace of God spread quickly, even reaching a seminarian in Poland fifteen years later, who wrote a booklet about him in Polish. This seminarian ultimately became St John Paul II. He declared Matt Talbot to be Venerable, a step on the road to his canonisation, in 1975 and wanted to visit Matt's tomb in the Church of Our Lady of Lourdes in Seán McDermott Street in Dublin when he visited Ireland in 1979, but was unable to do so. However, Pope Francis did make it to Seán Mac Dermott Street and venerated Matt Talbot's relics on his visit in 2018.

Lord, in your servant, Matt Talbot You have given us a wonderful example of triumph over addiction, of devotion to duty, and of lifelong reverence for the Most Holy Sacrament.

May his life of prayer and penance give us courage to take up our crosses and follow in the footsteps of Our Lord and Saviour, Jesus Christ.

Father, if it be Your will that Your beloved servant should be glorified by Your Church, make known by Your heavenly favours the power he enjoys in Your sight. We ask this through the same Jesus Christ Our Lord.
Amen.

Prayers and
Reflections
for Our Times

In this age of hi-tech gadgets and cyberspace, what relevance could a medieval saint possibly have for us? It is over eight hundred years since St Clare left home and began the Poor Clare Order along with St Francis. The following reflections and prayers are an attempt to introduce this extraordinary woman to the people of our times, and to look at ways in which she can continue to inspire us today.

In Times of Insecurity and Anxiety

In this time of great change, when so many things we took for granted are no longer certain, and the world seems to be out of control, we can marvel at how St Clare trusted that Jesus would always come through for her – He Himself was the Way, when it was unclear what would happen next. In response to a friar who was encouraging her to be patient during her final illness, she replied in a firm voice:

> *After I once came to know the grace of my Lord Jesus Christ through His servant Francis, no pain has been bothersome, no penance too severe, no weakness, dearly beloved brother, has been hard.*

What is striking is her courage, right to the end.
She lived trusting that '*by turning everything to their good God co-operates with all those who love him*' (Romans 8:28). In this spirit we pray.

In Times of Insecurity and Anxiety

Lord Jesus,
in these times of insecurity and anxiety,
we are stretched
in so many ways,
spiritually,
physically,
financially.
People are no longer given
their true dignity,
and so much that we treasure is gone.
It is hard at times to trust.
Help us to anchor ourselves in You,
whose love for us is unchanging.
May Your Spirit lead us in Your way.
May our hope in You give us
the peace of soul You promise.
Amen.

Pray for Guidance in Difficult Times

At the beginnings of St Clare's new religious community, the sisters had to contend with many difficulties. St Clare goes as far as outlining some of them in her rule – *'poverty, hard work, trial, shame and the contempt of the world'.*

When St Francis saw how well the sisters had coped with all their difficulties, he was very moved and he gave them a Form of Life, which was to be their guiding inspiration. In it he said they had *'… taken the Holy Spirit as a spouse'*, and it is clear from her life that St Clare had. This is an unusual term for a nun, as St John Paul II said in a letter to the Poor Clares, but he also said that it showed that there was a 'resonance' between her life and Luke's account of the Annunciation, when Our Lady was filled with the Holy Spirit.

The Holy Spirit strengthened Our Lady to deal with suffering in her life. And the Holy Spirit was the source of St Clare's inner strength too.

As she lay dying, St Clare spoke these words to her soul:

> *The One who created you has infused the Holy Spirit in you and then guarded you as a mother does her littlest child.*

PC 11:3

St Clare lived her life in the light of the Holy Spirit's grace and this sustained her in all her difficulties and carried her at this final hurdle. In this spirit, we pray a prayer written by St Francis (Lt Ord 50–52).

Prayer for Guidance in Difficult Times

This prayer was written by St Francis:

Almighty, eternal, just and merciful God,
Give us miserable ones
the grace to do for You alone
what we know You want us to do
and always to desire what pleases You.
Inwardly cleansed,
interiorly enlightened
and inflamed by the fire of the Holy Spirit,

may we be able to follow
in the footprints of Your beloved Son,
our Lord Jesus Christ,
and, by Your grace alone,
may we make our way to You,
Most High,
Who live and rule
in perfect Trinity and simple Unity,
and are glorified
God almighty,
forever and ever.
Amen.

When Our Fears
Overwhelm Us

We will all experience times when the fear within seems to engulf us. When this happens, it seems that we cannot see the way forward. We are often paralysed by these fears and anxieties. It is part of the human condition. Perhaps that is why one of the things we hear most in Scripture is *'Do not be afraid'* (Isaiah 43:1) or *'Do not let your hearts be troubled'* (John 14:1). It seems that God knows that we need to have it hammered home to us. He is stronger than our fears and He has conquered. We need only entrust ourselves to Him and we can claim His strength, which comes from the Holy Spirit.

St Clare had very little material security in her life. She faced huge obstacles bravely, trusting in God. In writing to her friend St Agnes of Prague and seeking to encourage her in the difficulties she was experiencing, she said (2 LAg 13–14):

Go forward
securely, joyfully and swiftly,
on the path of prudent happiness

believing nothing, agreeing with nothing
that would dissuade you from this commitment.
In this spirit we pray.

When Our Fears Overwhelm Us

Lord,
I am often filled with fear when I think of the future.
I am haunted by past mistakes and hurts,
afraid of what the future might hold
and I feel paralysed.
I surrender it all to You now.
I ask You to heal all that is wounded in me
and trust You to take care of all I worry about.
You are the One
who makes all things new.
With You I will go forward,
securely and joyfully,
into freedom.
Amen.

For Our Sense of Self-Esteem, Dignity and Worth

Today, self-fulfilment is of concern to many people – and, of course, it is important to develop ourselves to our full potential. However, if our focus is concentrated solely on ourselves, we will never find contentment, because a life that is self-centred is not a happy one. What is important is to try and find the balance between realising that everything we have received is a gift and, then, having the liberty to relax into enjoying this with a grateful heart, because Jesus came that we may have life to the full (John 10).

When St Clare was called by the Lord, she deliberately set out on a path that was uncertain, living a life of poverty that left her exposed and vulnerable. In this, she learned to depend on God to carry her. As she grew into this way of life and saw that the Lord actually did support her, she came to appreciate more and more how much she was loved. And it was this that nurtured her true self-worth, and gave her an inner strength that continued to grow. When the time came for her to die, she cried out, *'May You be blessed, O Lord, You who have created my soul'* (L Cl 46). It is very beautiful to

think that at the end of her life, she had no regrets and was happy to be who she was. It shows a great inner strength and harmony. And so we pray.

For Our Sense of Self-Esteem, Dignity and Worth

Lord,
You tell us in Scripture that we are precious in Your
eyes and that You love us (Isaiah 43:4).
Help us to truly believe this, so that we can come to
appreciate our true worth.
We seek happiness in many ways,
chasing the latest products,
thinking they will make us more acceptable.
And yet our hearts are created for greater things and
remain restless until they rest in You.
We ask You to heal the wounded areas of our hearts.
Help us to make a gift of ourselves to others,
so that we may find ourselves in this giving.
Let us appreciate our giftedness, so that we can come
to thank You for creating us.
Amen.

On the Grace of Work when Employed

St Clare was determined that the sisters would not earn revenue from property. Instead, she wanted the sisters to rely on the providence of God, keeping themselves by the work of their hands. She spoke of *'the grace of work'*, because she realised that to be able to work was, in itself, a great gift. When we can do something productive, it gives meaning to our lives.

The reality of life in their monastery was very difficult, with about fifty sisters living in a very cramped space, with no fixed income. What prevented this from disheartening them and reducing their existence to mere drudgery was the attitude that St Clare inspired in them. She stressed that they were to be employed in such a way that *'idleness, which is the enemy of the soul'* would be banished and which would not extinguish the *'spirit of prayer and devotion'*. For her, as for St Francis, this 'spirit of prayer and devotion' was the most important thing and everything else had to take a back seat. She saw their work as enabling them to return to the Lord an increase in the talents given by Him and so kept the Lord's goodness to them before their eyes constantly, as their incentive.

On the Grace of Work
when Employed

Lord, we thank You for the gifts You have given us.
We thank You especially for the grace of employment.
We thank You for the work that we do
and the people we work with.
We ask You to help us as we work,
so that we may apply ourselves to
the best of our ability.
When we struggle or feel stressed out,
or are just bogged down with the drudgery of it all,
help us to have a clear vision of purpose in our lives.
We pray for those who are unhappy in their work,
especially those who experience bullying.
May Your grace help and sustain them.
Amen.

The Grace of Work and Dealing with Unemployment

So many people cannot work, either because they cannot find work (which is a very big issue today) or because they are unable to work. St Clare appreciated that our dignity does not depend on what we do; it is the quality of our lives that matters. Every human being has an inherent dignity because we are made in the image and likeness of God. In this, she is a great witness to us today, when unemployment is so high. She knew the interior struggle of being unable to work because she was disabled for the last twenty-seven years of her life. This brought her into dependence on others, so she can empathise with us in our daily struggles.

St Clare outlined some of the difficulties that the community in San Damiano, which had about fifty sisters in it, had to struggle with – *'deprivation, poverty, hard work, trial, shame and the contempt of the world'.* As their leader, she was intensely aware of what was needed to provide for them all.

And, in the midst of all of that, she fell ill and remained bedridden for the remainder of her life. It is clear that, though not unemployed in the sense that we would look at it today, she experienced many of the things that those who are unemployed have to contend with – insecurity, the sense of not being able to contribute in the way that we would like to, not being able to exercise our abilities. In addition, there are the things she mentions herself – poverty, deprivation and shame.

Yet somehow, living in such dependence, she came to a serene acceptance of what was her lot. She saw that Christ was most powerful and accomplished the most when everything was stripped of Him on the Cross. She gained inspiration from that.

The Grace of Work
and Dealing with
Unemployment

Heavenly Father,
I thank You for the gifts that You have
given me for work,
especially for the gifts of health, strength and
the necessary talents.
You know how painful it is for me at this time,
not having the opportunity to put these gifts to use
in rewarding employment.

And so I ask You for the graces I need
to cope with unemployment.
I ask You to provide for my needs and those
who are dependent on me.
Help me when insecurity, fears and feelings of
uselessness rob me of peace
and help me to remember that my value as a person
doesn't depend
on whether or not I have a job.

*May I find employment in which I will find fulfilment
and contribute in a positive way to society.
I ask this in Jesus' name.
Amen.*

St Clare and
Healing the Sick

St Clare was a saint who knew the reality of sickness at first hand – she was bed-ridden for the last twenty-seven years of her life. According to the testimonies of her sisters, she bore her infirmity well and was a source of consolation and refuge for all of them. Not only that, the sisters came to her when they were finding it too difficult to cope with their own illnesses. Many of them testified that they were cured by her prayers.

St Francis also turned to her when healing was needed. He sent friars in need of healing to her for prayer and, when very ill himself, he came to San Damiano, the monastery of St Clare, in order to be taken care of.

At this time, when he was extremely sick, he wrote a canticle for the sisters in which he said, *'Those weighed down by sickness and the others wearied because of them, all of you: bear it in peace'* (Ct Exh 5).

Her own experience of illness enabled St Clare to respond with compassion for those suffering. And yet she encouraged them to see beyond the pain they were suffering. She wrote:

If you suffer with Him, you will reign with Him,
weeping with Him, you will rejoice with Him.

2 LAg 21

Confident of having someone who knows what the pain
of sickness involves, we ask her to pray for us now.

Prayer to
St Clare in Sickness

St Clare, lover of the poor Christ,
who bore your own sufferings with patience,
your trust in God's promises
helped you to keep going in your own suffering.
You lovingly tended the sick in your own monastery:
you were there for anyone who asked your help,
and interceded for them in their misery.
We ask you to intercede for us with Jesus,
who always heeded your prayers
and obtain for us the healing of which
we are in such need.
Amen.

Prayers for
Special Intentions

At different times in our lives we have special intentions that are close to our heart. Sometimes, we are not able to put these intentions into words. At such times, it is consoling to read in scripture: *'The Spirit too comes to help us in our weakness, so when we cannot choose words in order to pray properly, the Spirit Himself expresses our plea in a way that could never be put into words'* (Romans 8:26). However, it is helpful to be able to express these needs. We are often asked to pray for many of these intentions and we offer the following prayers to try to articulate some of them.

Anxiety in the Air

Therefore do not be anxious about tomorrow,
  for tomorrow will be anxious for itself.
Let the day's own trouble be sufficient for the day.
(Matthew 6:25)

The decade since this book was first published has been marked by technological progress that has made the pace of life so fast that we are catching up all the time, a global pandemic which threw the world into unprecedented upheaval, the outbreak of violence in many areas and the refugee crisis that accompanies war and unrest, not to mention environmental concerns. The accompanying disquiet is quite palpable. Anxiety almost seems to be in the air we breathe.

And many of us are finding it very hard to cope. One of the above concerns alone would be hard to deal with, but these have followed on in rapid succession and often overlapped each other.

Of all of the above, the Covid-19 pandemic is one that has impacted everyone, and its effects are still being felt. The enforced isolation that we had to live with for so long, along with the fear of contagion, meant that we were removed from many of the safety mechanisms that have always sustained us. Simple

social interactions like going for a cup of coffee with friends or attending Mass disappeared for a time. The Lord created us to love and care for each other, and these social interactions are an important part of how we nourish our relationships. Without them, our ability to cope with anxieties was seriously affected and we had to dig very deep for other ways to cope. For some, the ability to communicate has been badly damaged, compounding their pain.

In the absence of other outlets for our energies during the lockdowns, we became used to being fed with negative news and statistics. Many of us maintained that habit of monitoring the news constantly throughout the day. While it's important to have an awareness of the wider world, there is a correlation between receiving these constant updates and the anxiety problem, with the result that often the more information we receive, the more our anxiety can grow. We are also each dealing with the anxieties that occur in our own daily lives, ranging from worries about high electricity bills or upcoming doctor's appointments or a falling out we may have had with a friend.

And Jesus simply says to us *'Do not be anxious'*. (Matthew 6:34)

In fact, in the passage where He talks about this, He repeats this plea several times, because He knows how

debilitating anxiety is, affecting both our mental and physical health:

Therefore I tell you, do not be anxious about your life, what you shall eat or what you shall drink, nor about your body, what you shall put on. Is not life more than food, and the body more than clothing?

Look at the birds of the air: they neither sow nor reap nor gather into barns, and yet your heavenly Father feeds them. Are you not of more value than they?

And which of you by being anxious can add one cubit to his span of life?

And why are you anxious about clothing? Consider the lilies of the field, how they grow; they neither toil nor spin;

yet I tell you, even Solomon in all his glory was not arrayed like one of these.

But if God so clothes the grass of the field, which today is alive and tomorrow is thrown into the oven, will he not much more clothe you, O men of little faith?

Therefore do not be anxious, saying, 'What shall we eat?' or 'What shall we drink?' or 'What shall we wear?'

For the Gentiles seek all these things; and your heavenly Father knows that you need them all. But seek first his kingdom and his righteousness, and all these things shall be yours as well.

Therefore do not be anxious about tomorrow, for tomorrow will be anxious for itself. Let the day's own trouble be sufficient for the day.
(Matthew 6:25-34)

God does not wish for us to be anxious, but what can we do about our anxiety, especially when we are immersed in feelings of apprehension and the negative symptoms have already kicked in?

When Our Lord was struggling and in deep anguish during His prayer and agony in the Garden of Gethsemane, being human, He needed His friends to be close by. They were not able to give Him the support He needed at that point and yet their presence was a comfort to Him. But there are many other examples in Scripture where He clearly sought out the company of close friends and felt their support. Similarly, the Lord works through the people He puts in our lives.

Talking or sharing with a trusted friend or family member, a colleague, your priest or your doctor can be beneficial. Seeking professional help may be called for in certain situations when you are struggling. Speaking

to a counsellor and/or taking medication is an important part of living with anxiety for many people.

Day to day, some things that help us when we are feeling overwhelmed include getting out in the fresh air to take a brisk walk, doing something creative to slow down racing thoughts, and practising deep breathing.

While these practical steps are good and even essential when we are struggling with anxiety, bringing our cares to the Lord helps greatly. Jesus said:

'Come to me all you who labour and are overburdened and I will give you rest ... for I am gentle and humble of heart and you will find rest for your souls'
(Matthew 11: 28, 29b)

Bringing Anxiety to Prayer

The Spirit too comes to help us in our weakness. For when we cannot choose words in order to pray properly, the Spirit Himself expresses our plea in a way that could never be put into words, and God who knows everything in our hearts knows perfectly well what He means, and that the pleas of the saints expressed by the Spirit are according to the mind of God.
(Romans 8:26-27)

When we pray, we need to come before the Lord just as we are, otherwise we are not being honest with God, who is our healer. We do not need to wait until our minds are settled and calm in order to do this – instead we can look to God to help us find the calm and peace we need, relaxing in His presence as best we can, opening ourselves to His healing love.

Once you begin, use a prayer to call on the Holy Spirit – you could simply say, 'Come Holy Spirit, bring your healing grace' or another simple phrase in your own words. The Hebrew name for the Spirit is *Ruah*, which is the word for breath or wind, so the Holy Spirit is the breath of God. It is good to take a bit of time to notice your breathing and realise that our breath is a gift of God. Doing this helps us to calm down and as we inhale, we can ask the Holy Spirit to fill us.

Invite the Lord into the situation that's disturbing you and talk to Him about how you feel. Hand over to God any issue that may be preying on your mind. Then intentionally leave these things in His hands and don't dwell on them. If they come to mind again, gently hand them back to God if you become aware of them. St Peter tells us, *'unload all your worries on to him, since he is looking after you. Be calm but vigilant'* (1 Peter 5:7). You could read the section in this book on Surrender (page 36) to further understand how surrendering ourselves to our loving God can be liberating.

The antidote to anxiety is trust, so handing over our problems to God helps us to grow in trust. This is the basis of the Divine Mercy Devotion, for example. As part of this devotion Jesus revealed to St Faustina that He would like a new picture of Him to be painted which demonstrated His love for us. At the base of the picture the words *'Jesus I trust in you'* were to be written. To pray these words, or simply say the name of Jesus, helps this trust in God take root.

Alternatively, the daily prayer from the Novena of Surrender (which appears on page 245) is a lovely short prayer of trust: *'O Jesus I surrender myself to You, take care of everything'.* Praying some of the lines of Scripture given at the back of the book or using the 'Gaze Upon Him' prayer method described on page 28 could also work well.

Setting aside ten to fifteen minutes to do this, or thirty minutes if you have the time, should help. Indeed, cultivating time for daily quiet prayer, even if some days that time is very short, should help to calm your mind because Jesus is the source of our peace. It is best to sit in a comfortable chair and be relaxed when you take this time with the Lord. Being in a church or an adoration chapel can help to enter into a place of silence and calm within.

You can adapt the following prayer to suit your own needs at a particular time, or indeed change it if you are praying it for someone other than yourself.

Jesus,
You repeatedly say to us, 'Do not be anxious'
and 'Do not worry'.

I hear those words not so much as a command,
but rather as words which You speak to us
with loving concern.

You know how debilitating anxiety can
be and how pervasive it is.

There seems to be triggers for it everywhere.

You know my innermost being and can see
how it is impacting on me and my health.

I often do not know how to pray, but I beg You
come into my heart with Your healing balm.

I pray Your Holy Spirit will come into the very
deepest recesses of my mind and heart with
His healing grace.

Help me to say 'No' at times when I have too
much on my plate and help me to find ways to
cope with my anxiety that are wholesome, so that
I may experience the joy of Your saving help.

I ask this in Your Name.
Amen.

A Parent's Prayer

Dear Lord,

I thank You for the gift of my children. I thank You for the gift of faith that you have given me. I ask You to keep me faithful and to give me the grace to pass this on to them, so that they grow up loving You and knowing that they are loved by You.

Keep them safe. I worry so much about them sometimes, because the world in which we live today has so many dangers. I cannot possibly watch over them constantly, and so I ask You to do this. Give them good friends who will help them mature and develop into caring adults.

I thank You for their health and I ask You to give them continued good health. I know that they are precious in Your sight. I know that You love them even more than I do and so I entrust them to Your care. I consecrate myself and all my family to Your divine mercy.
Amen.

*L*et the little children come to me,
and do not stop them.

Luke 18:16

Prayer for Those
Unable to Sleep

Lord,

Please help me to sleep tonight. I find it so hard when I cannot sleep. The more I think about it, the more restless and anxious I get. It defeats the purpose, I know, but I can't seem to help it. I should go to bed because I need the sleep, but part of me dreads the long hours of darkness.

Let Your Holy Spirit fill me with Your peace, so that I can relax and get the sleep I need. And, if I cannot sleep, give me the deep serenity in my heart of knowing that I am loved by You and that You want me to rest in Your love.

Amen.

*U*nload all your worries on to Him,
since He is looking after you.

1 Peter 5:7

Prayer for Healing at Bedtime

Heavenly Father,
I thank You that You always take care of me.
Fill me with Your Holy Spirit.
There are so many areas where I need healing

(Pause for a moment to think of the areas that come to mind; particularly recall incidents that have occurred during the day)

Holy Spirit, let Your grace repair those areas now.
Heal the wounds I am not aware of,
especially things that are an obstacle to love of
 God and my neighbour.
Heavenly Father,
I repent of any ways that I have offended You,
 consciously or unconsciously.
As I settle down to sleep, I surrender it all to You.
I ask for the gift of a good night's sleep.
I trust that Your healing action will continue
 through the night because,
as the psalmist says …

*You pour gifts on Your beloved while they
  slumber. (Psalm 126)*

*I entrust myself and my family to Your mercy.
I ask all of this in Jesus' name.
Amen.*

Prayer for a
Parent with a Sick Child

Dear Lord,

I thank You for the precious gift of my child. I ask You to heal her. You know how much it upsets me to see her suffer. I feel so helpless, unable to take her pain away and I can do so little to help her. I beg You to bring relief to her. You are our loving Father and I believe that You therefore understand exactly how I feel.

Please help me to be what I should be in this situation and give me the grace to trust in You always. I believe that in Your will is our peace, but please help me to live this out, as I find it so hard when she is suffering. I entrust her to Your care. I ask this in Jesus' name. Amen.

*Jesus said, 'Do not be afraid; only have faith.'
Taking with Him the child's father and mother
and His own companions, He went into the
place where the child lay. And taking the child
by the hand, He said to her, 'Talitha, kum' which
means, 'Little girl, I tell you to get up.'*

Mark 36:40-41

Prayer for a Person Suffering from Illness

Dear Lord,

I ask You to heal me. I feel so wretched and it seems to be constant. When I am submerged by sickness, it takes over and I can think of nothing else. I ask You to lay Your healing hands on me and bring me some relief. I believe in Your power to heal, which You showed so much when You were on earth. I believe that You want only what is best for me, and so I ask You to give me the graces I need.

If it is not Your will that I be healed at this time, send Your Holy Spirit to comfort and strengthen me and use my suffering to somehow help others. I ask You especially to bless those who are looking after me. I trust in You and Your great love for me, and so I leave myself in Your hands.
Amen.

Lord, heal me, my body is racked:
my soul is racked with pain.

Psalm 6:2–3

Prayer for Those Who Don't Want to Miss Out on Anything

The fear of missing out (also known as FOMO) has become a distinct phenomenon in our times. So much is happening all the time and, with the advent of incessant posts on social media and digital devices constantly in our hands, we know a lot about what is happening around us, and without us all the time. In addition to consuming a lot of our precious time, consuming this information also feeds into the anxiety that many of us feel about not being good enough or that life is passing us by. This compulsion is leaving many people feeling discontent with their lives and unable to see what is good around them. It is important to step away and prioritise real connection – with God, with others, with ourselves – as a reminder of what really matters.

Lord,
Sometimes I feel overwhelmed at the pace of life
and feel as if I am constantly failing behind.
I catch myself persistently checking my phone,
wanting to know what is going on, rather than
savouring and enjoying my life, just as it is.
What is this obsession with keeping up with everyone
else's lives saying to me?
Why am I not content with simply enjoying my life?
I notice the more I flick from one post to another, the
less I am connected with what is really going on for
me, here and now.
In truth I know it actually feeds dissatisfaction and
this compulsive need to know everything is actually
impoverishing me, because feeling I am missing out
leaves me unhappy.
I pray for the grace to use social media in a more
positive way.
Free me from any way that I am controlled by my
devices so that I regain freedom in my life.
Let me hear in my heart the words You spoke to St
Paul: 'My grace is enough for you'.
Help me to recognise that You are the fulfilment of my
heart's deepest longings.
I ask this in Jesus' Name.
Amen.

Bullying

Bullying is not a new phenomenon. It is as old as humanity, portrayed even in the Old Testament. However, as society seems to move towards an 'anything-goes' mentality and away from a moral code which is built on the intrinsic value and dignity of every human being, it has become more prevalent.

While the widespread use of social media and the Internet can be used for great good, it seems to make tyrannising others easier. In the digital world, many fail to remember that they are communicating with real people and forget to approach conversations with kindness and respect.

Those who have a tendency to push others around are often in pain themselves but understanding this doesn't make the hurt they cause any easier to bear.

If you are experiencing the negative effects of intimidation and bullying (say at school or work) you can seek out help. It takes a lot of courage to do this in the face of the unnerving and threatening behaviour of the offender but it is good to keep in mind that everyone deserves to be treated with consideration and respect, and sharing what you are going through with a trusted person may help to lessen your burden.

In the meantime, bringing your hurt and pain to the Lord in prayer can help to alleviate the anxiety and fear surrounding what you're going through. Feel free to adapt this prayer according to your circumstances.

Heavenly Father,
I ask You to help me at this difficult time. I dread
going (here mention the relevant location e.g. online,
to work, to school, etc.) as it puts me into the
situation in which I am being treated unfairly.

The more I think about it the worse I feel, and the
anticipation of it can sometimes be worse than
the experience itself. My self-confidence has been
shattered and my spirit feels broken.

Help me to regain my sense of Your love for me, to
act as an anchor to keep me steady in the storm. I
pray for a change of heart for those responsible, that
they might begin to treat me with more respect and
recognise my dignity as Your child, known and loved
by You since before time began.

'Give me again the joy of Your help.
Rescue me, God my helper and my tongue s
hall ring out Your goodness.' (Ps 50)

I ask this in Jesus' name.
Amen.

For Those who Feel Lonely, Abandoned or Rejected

Dear Lord,

Sometimes I feel so lonely and seem to get engulfed by these feelings. The more I think about it, the more I get bogged down by it all. Let me experience Your deep love for me, so that I may be strengthened in my inner self. Let me find my security in You, so that, even when I am alone, I may not feel this dreadful loneliness.

I know that if this sense of being loved by You takes a deep root in my heart, my self-worth will return and I will find it easier to have the confidence to face situations in life that I often avoid now and which leave me feeling lonely. I ask you to heal me of this. I trust in You – let me not be disappointed.

Amen.

*Y*ou are precious in my eyes
and I love you.

Isaiah 43:4

Prayer for Those Struggling with Self-Hatred

Many of us struggle with a persistent sense that somehow we are not good enough or even, in very dark moments, that we are a waste of air and space.

Formative experiences can colour how we go through life. And when these are negative, such as comparing ourselves unfavourably to our siblings, criticism from teachers at school, or unkindness from friends, we can be left with a low opinion of ourselves. Even parents, most of whom are doing their best, can make mistakes as they raise their children and contribute to these feelings, even if they don't mean to. And at this young age, we do not yet have the perspective we need to stand back and process in a healthy way these negative experiences and the feelings they provoke.

Of course, negative experiences can happen at any age unfortunately, and some can be very traumatic and difficult for us to process without help. The resulting feelings can develop into negative thought patterns, which perpetuate them, and modern society often does not help us here. For example, in an age governed by images, as our digital world is, we can find ourselves

filled with self-hate, a potentially destructive state of mind, if we do not meet societal expectations of what we should look like. Yet scripture tells us:

God does not see as man sees; man looks at appearances but the Lord looks at the heart.
(1 Samuel 16:7)

But how do we counteract these feelings, which can often feel very overwhelming? Removing negative influences from our lives, whether this is distancing ourselves from friends who treat us poorly or unfollowing social media accounts that make us feel bad about ourselves, is a good place to start. But we also need to change the things we say to ourselves about ourselves.

Sr Concilio, a Mercy sister who founded the Cuan Mhuire addiction treatment centres around the country, has visited our community a few times. On one occasion she suggested following a practice to cultivate a better understanding of our inherent goodness as children of God. Her advice is to say these words often during the day:

I am good
I was always good
God made me good.

And we could add these liberating words of the Psalm, which make this a prayer of gratitude:

I thank You for the wonder of my being.
(Psalm 139:14)

These words seem very simple. But how often do we tell ourselves the opposite without thinking? By switching gears and reminding ourselves that we are good, we can help to neutralise the impact of those lies. In the book of Genesis, it is written that when God created nature, He said 'it is good'. But when he made man and woman, He said they were 'very good'. God made us in a way that reflects the utter goodness of God and He delights in us, just as we are. This is the original blessing. Furthermore, Genesis also tells us we are made in the image of God which emphasises how precious we are in His eyes. This is the source of our belovedness.

A key approach to our healing is to cultivate gratitude. By thanking God for all He has given us, including our existence, we are inviting His healing power into our lives and it is liberating. One of the more popular psalms, Psalm 139 (quoted above), helps us put words on a conversation that we can have with the Lord. Jesus has revealed how much we are loved by God, so this Psalm emphasises gratitude to God for the possibility of intimacy with Him.

There are many other beautiful thoughts in this psalm, which illustrate how greatly we are treasured by God. It would be a worthwhile practice to regularly take time to quieten down with the Lord and to pray Psalm 139, from the heart. It is reproduced on page 280 of this book.

And we give a shorter prayer with this intention in mind here:

O Lord
You know me intimately, because You 'knit me
together in my mother's womb' (Ps 139:13).

From all eternity You chose to create me.
You have made me good and I thank You for the
wonder of my being (Ps 139:14)

Heal me in all the areas where I have been damaged
and impress on my spirit the truth
that I am 'precious in Your eyes and You love me'
(Isaiah 43:4)

I ask this in Jesus' Name.
Amen.

Prayer for People with Suicidal Thoughts

Lord,

I beg You to help me with Your grace. I feel so desperate and am so burdened at this time that I can see no way out of the rut I am in. My whole life seems to be crumbling around me and I feel that I cannot go on. I know deep down that You have created all life and that it is sacred, but it feels like life is no longer worth living. I know, too, that You have created me and love me and that You came that we may have life and have it to the full.

Please help me to experience that, as I seem to be struggling to exist at the moment. I beg You to allow Your love for me to penetrate the darkness that I am living in, because I know that it has the power to change me. Let Your Holy Spirit fill me with hope for the future and give me the security that I crave. I entrust myself to Your divine mercy.

Amen.

As soon as Peter felt the force of the wind, he took
fright and began to sink.
'Lord! Save me!'
Jesus put His hand out at once
and held him.

Matthew 14:30–31

Prayer for Those
Bereaved through Suicide

Lord,

I ask You to have mercy on all those who have taken their life and especially on _____
You alone know what burdens he was carrying. I ask You to forgive anything that needs to be forgiven and to let him enjoy eternal happiness with You. I ask You to give us the graces we need at this time as we struggle to come to terms with our loss. Nothing we have ever lived through could have prepared us for this.

Even as we try to cope with this loss, help us to overcome the deep, gnawing sense of guilt that we feel – even though we know that this feeling, that maybe there was something more we could have done, is senseless. I ask You to heal and strengthen us and bring us through these difficult times. I find great comfort in knowing that You are the Good Shepherd and that, even as we go through this dark valley, we do not need to be afraid, because You are with us and will comfort us (Psalm 22).

Amen.

He will wipe away all tears from their eyes;
there will be no more death, and no more
mourning or sadness, because the former
things have passed away.

Revelation 21:4

Prayer in Bereavement

Heavenly Father,
I come to You for consolation in my loss.

I don't know how to pray, nor do I really feel like praying.

I am only conscious of the deep pain in my heart, which is caused by my great loss.

I wish I could get beyond this pain, but each day brings reminders of _____ whom I love and who has now died.

I know that Your mercy is boundless and so I entrust _____ to You now.

My faith gives me the consolation of knowing that _____ is still close to me.

In You and by our prayers, we can still express our love for each other and help each other.

But the reality in my day to day life, is that I am lonely and miss _____

Please fill me with Your grace and consolation, and heal my pain-filled heart.

Give comfort to all the other people who are also grieving at this time.

I ask this in the name of Jesus.

Amen.

Prayer for Those Who have Died

Eternal rest grant unto her O Lord
and let perpetual light shine upon her.
May her soul and the souls of all the faithful departed,
through the mercy of God rest in peace.
Amen.

Additional Prayer when There are Regrets

We often have regrets when someone close to us dies – things we should have said or done. We often mull over them in our minds and it can prevent us from moving on and letting the person go.

We have purposely chosen to add a prayer for regrets, separately.

Dear Lord,
Since this death, I often have regrets.
Sometimes I think of things I should have said or done.
They might not be very big, but now it seems too late.
I know it is not helpful, but sometimes I can't stop myself regretting and it can be unsettling.
So I now surrender all to You.
I believe that with You all things are possible and that in You they are aware of my sorrow.
Come into the situation and bring healing.
I ask this in the name of Jesus.
Amen.

I understand the grief of people who have to endure
great suffering, yet slowly but surely we all have
to let the joy of faith slowly revive as a quiet yet
firm trust, even amid the greatest distress:
'My soul is bereft of peace; I have forgotten what
happiness is … But this I call to mind, and therefore
I have hope: the steadfast love of the Lord never
ceases, his mercies never come to an end; they are
new every morning. Great is your faithfulness …
It is good that one should wait quietly for the
salvation of the Lord'

(Lam 3:17, 21-23, 26)

Pope Francis, 'The Joy of the Gospel', paragraph 6

Some Prayers and Reflections to Accompany those who are Dying

When we are confronted with death, it is the ultimate experience of coming face to face with our poverty and helplessness. Whether it is our own death, or the death of someone we love, circumstances are out of our control and it can be frightening. God's Word is all embracing at a time like this, as it expresses His compassionate presence and power. It is incisive and works in a mysterious, yet real way.

When we are facing our own death, we may find it difficult to pray. And yet, that is the very time when we would like to be able to communicate with God, but may not know how or where to start.

Similarly, if we are with someone in their last days or hours, we may feel helpless. We long to give them some comfort and reassurance to support them in their final journey. We may be unsure of how to pray, particularly if we are not used to praying.

The following reflections and prayers, interspersed with Scriptural quotations, are offered as a way of

dialoguing with the Lord at this lonely time. They are written as one would pray them for oneself. However, they may be prayed in the same way on behalf of someone else. Given that the sense of hearing continues, even when other senses have failed, it may give great comfort to the one listening, who may not be able to articulate the prayers. You are lending them your voice to facilitate their conversation with God.

Jesus, You have said,
Do not let your hearts be troubled
Trust in God still, and trust in me.
There are many rooms in My Father's house;
if there were not, I should have told you.
I am going now to prepare a place for you,
and after I have gone and prepared you a place
I shall return to take you with me;
so that where I am
you may be too.
(John 14:1–3)

Jesus, I believe in Your Word and that You are faithful to Your Word. Therefore, I place all my trust in you now. I believe that You have gone to prepare a special place for me, in Your Father's house. I long to go there, to be freed to live fully in You. And yet, there is fear in me; not so much a fear of You, but fear of the unknown, a fear of letting go. And I feel for those I am leaving behind.

Be with me and take me by the hand and lead me to the Father.

Jesus, we recall the story of the good thief on the Cross and the wonderful promise You made to him.

> *'Jesus,' he said, 'remember me when You come into Your kingdom.'*
> *And You replied, 'Indeed, I promise You, today you will be with Me in Paradise.'*
> (Luke 23:49)

Jesus, I can only imagine the reassurance this brought to this condemned criminal. It is a source of great comfort to me at this time, that You are so merciful. In my struggle, between life and death, I too appeal to you, 'Jesus, remember me; be with me, strengthen me, so that I can go in peace.'

> *Come to my help, for I am alone and have no one but you, Lord.*
> *Free me from my fear.*
> (Esther 4:17t and 17z)

Sometimes the fears just well up in me and I feel overcome. Strengthen me, be with me, Jesus, my Saviour. Take away the anxieties that sap my energy and choke my trust.

Jesus, I trust in You. I may not feel that, but still I will continue to repeat it, hoping that trust in You will take deep root in me. Let my every breath say, "Jesus I trust in You, Jesus I trust in You". I need You now. Come, Lord Jesus, come.

The Lord is my Shepherd;
there is nothing I shall want.
Fresh and green are the pastures
where He gives me repose.
Near restful waters He leads me,
to revive my drooping spirit.

He guides me along the right path;
He is true to His Name.
If I should walk in the valley of darkness
no evil would I fear.
You are there with Your crook and Your staff;
with these You give me comfort.

You have prepared a banquet for me
in the sight of my foes.
My head You have anointed with oil
my cup is overflowing.

Surely goodness and kindness shall follow me
all the days of my life.
In the Lord's own house shall I dwell
forever and ever.
(Psalm 22/23)

This Psalm is a source of comfort and consolation to me. I ask You Father, to revive my drooping spirit now. Be with me in this dark valley, as You have promised, You who are true to Your name, You who are ever faithful. I trust that You are always with me, and so there is nothing to fear.

Help me to focus on the banquet that You have prepared for me, rather than on my present sufferings and my sins. And in Your mercy lead me safely to Your own house, that I may dwell there with You forever.

'Blessed those who die in the Lord! Blessed indeed, the Spirit says; now they can rest for ever after their work, since their good deeds go with them' (Rev 14:13).

Lord, as I approach the end of my life, I realise how few 'good deeds' I have. My life seems to have gone by so fast. In my own way, I think I tried to live a good life, to be kind. But, it seems so little now and there are regrets about what I could or should have done.

At this time, it is Your great mercy that gives me comfort and hope, because mercy loves and forgives when it is not deserved. So this fills me with confidence. I come to You with empty hands, trusting in Your merciful love.

I trust You; let me not be disappointed.

Because you have come to give Your people:

> *knowledge of salvation*
> *through the forgiveness of their sins;*
> *this by the tender mercy of our God*
> *who from on high will bring the rising Sun to visit*
> * us,*
> *to give light to those who live in darkness and the*
> * shadow of death,*
> *and to guide our feet into the way of peace.*
> (Luke 1: 77–79)

> *Now, Master, you can let your servant go in peace,*
> * just as you promised;*
> *because my eyes have seen the salvation which*
> * you have prepared for all the nations to see,*
> *a light to enlighten the pagans*
> *and the glory of your people Israel.*
> (Luke 2:29–32)

May He support us all the day long, till the shades lengthen, and the evening comes, and the busy world is hushed, and the fever of life is over, and our work is done.

> *'Then in His mercy may He give us a safe lodging,*
> *and a holy rest, and peace at the last.'*
> Blessed John Henry Newman

An Act of Contrition

It has always been considered important to say the Act of Contrition in the face of death. If one is with someone who is dying, it is a commendable practice to whisper an Act of Contrition into the ear of the dying person. An Act of Contrition is given on page 64.

Many of the other prayers given in the book are ideal for praying with someone who is dying. Particularly suitable prayers are:

Prayer for Those Suffering with Depression

Lord,

You know the darkness that envelops me. This cloud descends on me and, when it does, I seem to lose all perspective. It seems like it will never lift. I know I have pulled out of it before, but when it starts again, it clouds everything. Help me to trust in You in this difficult time. I know that after the rain, the sun shines again and that above the clouds, the sun is always shining.

But please impress this conviction in my heart, so that Your gift of hope will carry me through. I believe that You can heal me and so I entrust myself to You. Give me the graces I need to 'hang in there' until Your healing Love, which I know is constantly working on me, finally penetrates and gives me the relief that I need.

Amen.

*Out of His infinite glory, may He give you
the power through His Spirit for your hidden
self to grow strong.*

Ephesians 3:16

Prayer for
Expectant Mothers

Lord,

I thank You for the gift of new life and especially for the child in my womb. I ask You to bless him or her so that the child will grow up in the way that You would wish. I also ask that my child will be healthy in every way and will grow to love You in his or her life.

I ask that You give me good health, especially during my pregnancy, and that You will see that all goes well for both of us during childbirth.

Amen.

*For it was You who created my being,
knit me together in my mother's womb.
I thank You for the wonder
of my being.*

Psalm 138–139:13–14

Prayer for Those who Long to Have a Child

Lord,

You know the deepest longings of our hearts and how much we would love to have a child. We know every child is a gift from You. You know that we would cherish that child so much and that we long to have the joy of giving life in this deep sense.

If it is your will, Lord, we ask You to bless our marriage by giving us the gift of a child. If this is not to be, give us the grace to accept what is Your will with love. Show us other ways to express the fruitfulness of our married love, and be Yourself the fullness of our love.

Amen.

O *God, hear my cry!*
Listen to my prayer.

Psalm 60–61:1

Prayer for Those with an Unplanned Pregnancy

Lord,

You know the fears that are in my heart just now, as I carry a child within me. You know I hadn't planned this and that I am really struggling. I beg You for Your grace to come to terms with the reality of it all. I know in my heart of hearts that each new life is a gift from You, to be cherished. Give me the grace to do just that, because I am finding it so hard just now.

Please support me with Your grace so that I keep firm in my resolution to keep this child. Give me the material support that I will need in order to do so and put the right people in my path to help me. Bless and protect the child in my womb, so that he or she will be healthy and grow up in Your care.

Amen.

Do not worry about tomorrow: tomorrow will take care of itself. Each day has enough trouble of its own.

Matthew 6:34

Prayer for Those Suffering Addictions

Lord,

You know the anguish that engulfs me. You have seen the spiral of horror in my life, the way my addiction consumes me and has taken over completely. You know I hate what I am doing to my family and friends, as they look on helplessly. It causes me such deep pain, and yet I seem to be totally unable to just kick the habit and start afresh.

Please, please help me. I seem to live for the 'high', but it is all so empty and meaningless and sometimes I just despair. Give me hope and the courage to change. Give my family the graces they need to cope. You have said that You came that we would have life to the full. Let me be open to this through the power of Your Holy Spirit.

Amen.

For God, everything is possible.

Matthew 19:26

Prayer for Those in Financial Difficulty

Lord,

You know how difficult it is to make ends meet. Everything seems to be so expensive and it is a constant struggle to keep going.

Help me to have hope and provide for us so that I will be less consumed by this gnawing fear that is always with me. Help me to trust You to do this for us.

Amen.

We are in difficulties on all sides,
but never cornered;
we see no answer to our problems,
but never despair.

2 Corinthians 4:8

Prayer on Getting Older

A fact of life for all of us is that we are getting older. In a world that idolises youth and beauty that can bring a particular pain, making some of us feel excluded, lonely or even that we are becoming or have become useless. And yet we know that the longer we live, the more wisdom we have gained which we can offer to others for their benefit.

In a letter he addressed to grandparents and the elderly for World Grandparents Day, Pope Francis explored this idea. He said, 'No one prepares us for old age, and at times it seems to take us by surprise'. It is so obvious but true. Life prepares us for many things and particularly for being independent, but gradually our facility to do things can diminish and we start to slow down. We feel this keenly, as it is so opposed to the way we are used to living our lives. And as we get older, we can also feel left behind as the pace of the world around us speeds up.

Using the word 'we' to include himself among the elderly – a beautiful touch – Pope Francis speaks about the important role of this group in modern society, saying that they have a great responsibility to teach

others with the same loving approach as they would teach their own grandchildren: 'We ourselves have grown in humanity by caring for others, and now we can be teachers of a way of life that is peaceful and attentive to those in greatest need.'

It is good for older people to remember that there is much that can be learned from younger family members and friends. In reaching out to them the possibility of mutual enrichment can be discovered and enjoyed.

While wisdom is a great treasure to have gained over the course of a life, the greatest contribution that older people and grandparents can make is to be a safe and loving presence for others, being an example of faith and prayer within their family and community circles. Pope Francis captures this well:

Dear grandparents, dear elderly persons, we are called to be artisans of the revolution of tenderness in our world! Let us do so by learning to make ever more frequent and better use of the most valuable instrument at our disposal and, indeed, the one best suited to our age: prayer. Our trustful prayer can do a great deal: it can accompany the cry of pain of those who suffer, and it can help change hearts.

Encouraged by Pope Francis' conviction of the power of our prayer and conscious too that perhaps we are in need of being tender towards ourselves, we offer this prayer as way of bringing before the Lord the challenges we face in appreciating the giftedness of this stage of our lives.

Prayer on Getting Older

Dear Lord
At times I find it hard to face the reality of getting
older and the uncertainty of what lies in the future.
In my mind and heart, I feel twenty years younger than
I am and I eagerly embrace life.
Sometimes, though, when I go to move, the creaks
and aches tell a different story and I know that
physically I am not as quick as I used to be or as able
to do all the things I used to take for granted.
Also, I often feel overlooked and unimportant.
Younger people seem to have more zest for life and
capable of achieving more.
I compare and I shouldn't.

Help me to remember that my feelings of inadequacy are unfounded,
Please help me when at times these feelings threaten to overwhelm me, times when feelings of envy eat away at me.
Give me a more positive frame of mind about the gifts hidden in my older age.
I trust that You are with me and that You love me as I am. Help me to love myself as I am and to live life to the full (John 10:10), because that is why You came.
Amen.

Prayer for
Peace of Mind

O Jesus,

Banish from my mind all anxieties, troubles and fears of any kind. Make my mind calm and serene and fill it only with loving thoughts and confidence in You.

Amen.

When cares increase in my heart,
Your consolation calms my soul.

Psalm 93–94:19

Prayer for a Loving Marriage Partner

Heavenly Father,

The deepest desire of my heart is to meet someone with whom I can share love. I would really love to get married, to meet someone who could be a true soul-mate, someone I could love and cherish, as I wish to be loved myself.

It seems so hard today. People are afraid of commitment and, in truth, there is some fear in my own heart.

So I ask You, Lord, to grant this desire of my heart and let Your grace and love grow in me. I ask this in Jesus' name.

Amen.

If you find your delight in the Lord, He will grant you your heart's desire.

Psalm 36–37:4

Prayer for Those with Marital Difficulties

Heavenly Father,

I thank You for my marriage partner, for the gift of our married life together.

At this point in time, as You know, we are struggling. It can be so painful at times – to be living so closely with someone and yet unable to communicate in a constructive way.

I ask You to come into the situation. You are the third person in our marriage and we need Your grace to continue on.

Let Your Spirit of love and reconciliation renew and deepen our love for each other and help us to grow in trust.

We ask this in Jesus' name.
Amen.

*Love is always ready to excuse,
to trust, to hope and to endure
whatever comes.*

1 Corinthians 13:7

On Engaging With the Internet

As enclosed contemplative sisters, engagement with the Internet has always been a source of tension for us as we try to ensure it is used in a manner that does not weaken the structures of our daily life of prayer. Pope Francis issued guidelines specifically for our way of life some years ago when he counselled us to use the internet for 'formation and necessary communication' and to avoid 'wasting time' on it. We try to put this wisdom into practice as we use the Internet so that we can share the fruits of our way of life with others, for example through sharing prayers on our externally-managed Facebook page, while maintaining a balanced approach so as not become too distracted by it.

According to a more recent document from the Vatican with a general focus titled *Towards Full Presence: A Pastoral Reflection on Engagement with Social Media* 'the question is no longer whether to engage with the digital world but how'. The Good Samaritan is held up as a model for respecting and reverencing those we may encounter on the Internet, people who are complete strangers to us as the Good Samaritan was to the man he came upon lying half-dead on the road. The following prayer is inspired by some of our thoughts on that document:

Heavenly Father,
My smartphone has become an integral part of my
day-to-day life. There are so many ways that it is
useful and informative, connecting me to others who
share my interests and views.
At other times I feel that it can rob me of serenity and
peace, especially when I fall into comparing myself
negatively with others. May I never forget the truth
that I am precious in Your eyes.
Preserve me from Internet addictions and from being
deceived by fake news, images and videos that
contribute to the objectification and exploitation of
my brothers and sisters since we are all one family in
You and Your beloved daughters and sons.
In the spirit of the Gospel, grant me the wisdom to
know when to speak and when to remain silent in
online discussions, and to communicate at all times in
a spirit of love and openness with those whose views
may differ from mine.
Even though there is so much good on the Internet,
where I can learn much about You, I also need Your
help to find the freedom to take a break from social
media at times in order to pray, reflect and enjoy time
with You and with other people, especially those who
are dear to me.
I ask this in Jesus' Name.
Amen.

Preparing for Exams

In exams, much depends on our performance over a period of a few intense hours. Keeping a calm mind is half the battle in recalling what we have studied and giving a good performance.

To be able to centre yourself for a few minutes before starting to study or even to stop for a brief pause is a great help. Even the few minutes sitting at the desk before the exam actually starts can be used profitably to become relaxed.
We offer the following exercise to help release the tension and calm the mind:

Close your eyes.

Take a few deep breaths. As you inhale, silently say, 'Come, Holy Spirit, inspire me.'

The Holy Spirit is the breath of God and the One who is the source of all our inspirations. As you pray this, imagine the Holy Spirit coming in to do this within you.

Exhaling slowly, silently say, 'Release the tension, bring Your peace.'

As you pray this, feel the Holy Spirit drive the tension from your body.

This can be simplified to say 'Come, Holy Spirit' on inhalation and 'Bring Your peace' on exhalation.

Prayer for Those Sitting Exams

Lord,

I ask You to help me at this stressful time. I feel that so much depends on these exams. I feel that in addition to carrying my own burdens, I am carrying the expectations of so many others – family, friends, society.

Help me to keep calm at this time, so that I can think straight and apply myself to the best of my ability. Let Your Spirit help and inspire me, so that I can remember all that I have studied and put together my answers in the best way. Guide me in all my ways, so that I will find fulfilment in You.

Amen.

Let Your good spirit guide me.

Psalm 142–143:10

Prayer for Students
Taking Exams

Lord,

I ask you to send Your Spirit to inspire _____ in her studies. Help her to be attentive and alert. Help her to study the right topics. Inspire her during her exam so that she will stay calm and perform to the best of her ability.

I pray also that, in her quest for knowledge, she will come to know You and Your great love for her.

Amen.

*There is nothing I cannot master
with the help of the One
who gives me strength.*

Philippians 4:13

Final Prayer: to Experience God's Love for Us

As we conclude our reflections, we leave you with some words from the inaugural homily of Pope Benedict XVI.

Are we not perhaps all afraid in some way? If we let Christ enter fully into our lives, if we open ourselves totally to him, are we not afraid that He might take something away from us? Are we not perhaps afraid to give up something significant, something unique, something that makes life so beautiful? Do we not then risk ending up diminished and deprived of our freedom?

No! If we let Christ into our lives, we lose nothing, nothing, absolutely nothing of what makes life free, beautiful and great. No! Only in this friendship are the doors of life opened wide.

Do not be afraid of Christ! He takes nothing away and He gives you everything. When we give ourselves to Him, we receive a hundredfold in return. Yes, open, open wide the doors to Christ – and you will find true life.
Amen.

We hope that this book has given you a way of coming closer to the Lord. We hope that you will come to experience, in a full and deep way, God's all-embracing love for you. A prayer that beautifully expresses the fullness that is possible was written by St Paul, found in the third chapter of the letter to the Ephesians. This is our prayer for you:

This, then, is what I pray, kneeling before the Father,
from whom every family, whether spiritual
or natural, takes its name.

Out of His infinite glory, may He give you the power
through His Spirit for your hidden self to grow strong,
so that Christ may live in your hearts through faith,
and then, planted in love and built on love,
you will with all the saints have the strength to grasp
the breadth and the length, the height and the depth;
until, knowing the love of Christ, which is beyond
all knowledge, you are filled with the utter
fullness of God.

Glory be to Him, whose power, working in us, can
do infinitely more than we can ask or imagine.
Amen.

May the Lord bless you and keep you.
May He show His face to you and have mercy on you.
May He turn His countenance to you and
give peace to you.

The Blessing of St Clare

Further Reading
and Reflections

Prayer to Our Lady, Untier of Knots

Pope Francis has been promoting prayer to Our Lady under this title ever since he first saw a painting entitled 'Mary, Untier of Knots' (also sometimes known as 'Undoer of Knots') in Augsberg in the south of Germany, where he studied in the 1980s. It depicts Our Lady holding the ribbon of our lives. An angel is handing this ribbon to her and as she works through it, she unties all the knots, which symbolise the problems in our lives, so that the ribbon is smooth as it leaves her hands.

Pope Francis was in Germany at a particularly difficult period in his life and this concept of giving Our Lady the problems in our lives to sort out appealed very much to him and was a great source of support. When he returned to Argentina, he had prayer cards made featuring the painting, encouraging people to pray to Our Lady in troubling times. Since becoming Pope, he has spread this message throughout the world.

It is comforting to us to know that when we entrust the troubles of our lives into Our Lady's loving hands,

she will take care of them. She will help us to untie the knots. We all have concerns that overwhelm us and often seem out of our control. As Pope Francis has said, 'Those are the ones that are out of our hands, the knots of selfishness and indifference, economic and social knots, knots of violence and war.' But her motherly care embraces us and comes to our aid to help us find peace and remind us of God's love.

There are many prayers to Our Lady, Untier of Knots – this one was said by Pope Francis at the end of a month-long global rosary in May 2021:

> *O Mary, you, who know how to untie*
> *the knots of our existence,*
> *and know the desires of our hearts,*
> *come to our aid.*
> *We are certain that, as in Cana of Galilee,*
> *you will ensure that joy and celebration*
> *will return to our homes after this time of trial.*
>
> *Help us, Mother of Divine Love,*
> *to conform ourselves to the will of the Father*
> *and to do what Jesus will tell us*
> *who took upon Himself our sufferings*
> *and took upon Himself our sorrows to lead us,*
> *through the cross, to the joy of the resurrection.*
> *Amen.*

The Novena of Surrender

This particular devotion is something that has come to our attention in recent years. Consisting of short, encouraging reflections for each day, its appeal lies very much in its simplicity.

Fr Don Dolindo Ruotolo (1882-1970) was a Neapolitan priest who had extraordinary communications with Jesus throughout his life. He received this devotion from Jesus over the course of nine days and it teaches us about total abandonment to God and trusting in His love for us.

Having found the novena extremely comforting and helpful when in situations which are out of our control, we have taken to spreading the word about it by distributing it to those who reach out to us for prayer. The reaction has been enormously positive – at the time of writing, we have just received a letter from someone who is finding this novena very helpful in a time of need. Somehow, it seems to anchor people and keep them steady in the turmoil.

If you find yourself in an overwhelming or daunting situation in which you need an anchor or if you find

it hard to 'let go and let God', you might find, as we have, that these daily reflections help put into words what perhaps we do not have words for and that in surrendering our problems to God, our burdens are lightened and we experience His peace.

The Novena of Surrender to the Will of God

Day 1

Why do you confuse yourselves by worrying? Leave the care of your affairs to me and everything will be peaceful. I say to you in truth that every act of true, blind, complete surrender to me produces the effect that you desire and resolves all difficult situations.

O Jesus, I surrender myself to You, take care of everything! (Repeat this line 10 times)

Concluding Prayer: Mother, I am yours now and forever. Through you and with you I always want to belong completely to Jesus.

Day 2

Surrender to me does not mean to fret, to be upset, or to lose hope, nor does it mean offering to me a worried prayer asking me to follow you and change your worry into prayer.

It is against this surrender, deeply against it, to worry, to be nervous and to desire to think about the consequences of anything.

It is like the confusion that children feel when they ask their mother to see to their needs, and then try to take care of those needs for themselves so that their childlike efforts get in their mother's way.

Surrender means to placidly close the eyes of the soul, to turn away from thoughts of tribulation and to put yourself in my care, so that only I act, saying 'You take care of it'.

O Jesus, I surrender myself to You, take care of everything! (Repeat this line 10 times)

Concluding Prayer: Mother, I am yours now and forever. Through you and with you I always want to belong completely to Jesus.

Day 3

How many things I do when the soul, in so much spiritual and material need, turns to me, looks at me and says to me 'You take care of it', then closes its eyes and rests. In pain you pray for me to act, but that I act in the way you want. You do not turn to me; instead, you want me to adapt to your ideas. You are not sick people who ask the doctor to cure you, but rather sick people who tell the doctor how to.

So do not act this way but pray as I taught you in the Our Father: 'Hallowed be thy Name', that is, be glorified in my need. 'Thy kingdom come', that is, let all that is in us and in the world be in accord with your kingdom. 'Thy will be done on Earth as it is in Heaven', that is, in our need, decide as you see fit for our temporal and eternal life. If you say to me truly 'Thy will be done', which is the same as saying 'You take care of it', I will intervene with all my omnipotence, and I will resolve the most difficult situations.

O Jesus, I surrender myself to You, take care of everything! (Repeat this line 10 times)

Concluding Prayer: Mother, I am yours now and forever. Through you and with you I always want to belong completely to Jesus.

Day 4

You see evil growing instead of weakening? Do not worry. Close your eyes and say to me with faith: 'Thy will be done, You take care of it.' I say to you that I will take care of it, and that I will intervene as does a doctor and I will accomplish miracles when they are needed. Do you see that the sick person is getting worse? Do not be upset, but close your eyes and say: 'You take care of it.' I say to you that I will take care of it, and that there is no medicine more powerful than my loving intervention. By my love, I promise this to you.

O Jesus, I surrender myself to You, take care of everything! (Repeat this line 10 times)

Concluding Prayer: Mother, I am yours now and forever. Through you and with you I always want to belong completely to Jesus.

Day 5

And when I must lead you on a path different from the one you see, I will prepare you; I will carry you in my arms; I will let you find yourself, like children who have fallen asleep in their mother's arms, on the other bank of the river.

What troubles you and hurts you immensely are your reason, your thoughts and worry, and your desire at all costs to deal with what afflicts you.

O Jesus, I surrender myself to You, take care of everything! (Repeat this line 10 times)

Concluding Prayer: Mother, I am yours now and forever. Through you and with you I always want to belong completely to Jesus.

Day 6

You are sleepless; you want to judge everything, direct everything and see to everything and you surrender to human strength, or worse – to men themselves, trusting

in their intervention. This is what hinders my words and my views.

Oh how much I wish from you this surrender, to help you and how I suffer when I see you so agitated! Satan tries to do exactly this: to agitate you and to remove you from my protection and to throw you into the jaws of human initiative.

So, trust only in me, rest in me, surrender to me in everything.

O Jesus, I surrender myself to You, take care of everything! (Repeat this line 10 times)

Concluding Prayer: Mother, I am yours now and forever. Through you and with you I always want to belong completely to Jesus.

Day 7

I perform miracles in proportion to your full surrender to me and to your not thinking of yourselves. I sow treasure troves of graces when you are in the deepest poverty. No person of reason, no thinker, has ever performed miracles, not even among the saints. He does divine works whosoever surrenders to God.

So don't think about it anymore, because your mind is acute and for you it is very hard to see evil and to trust in me and to not think of yourself. Do this for all

your needs, do this all of you and you will see great continual silent miracles. I will take care of things, I promise this to you.

O Jesus, I surrender myself to You, take care of everything! (Repeat this line 10 times)

Concluding Prayer: Mother, I am yours now and forever. Through you and with you I always want to belong completely to Jesus.

Day 8
Close your eyes and let yourself be carried away on the flowing current of my grace; close your eyes and do not think of the present, turning your thoughts away from the future just as you would from temptation.

Repose in me, believing in my goodness, and I promise you by my love that if you say 'You take care of it', I will take care of it all; I will console you, liberate you and guide you.

O Jesus, I surrender myself to You, take care of everything! (Repeat this line 10 times)

Concluding Prayer: Mother, I am yours now and forever. Through you and with you I always want to belong completely to Jesus.

Day 9

Pray always in readiness to surrender, and you will receive from it great peace and great rewards, even when I confer on you the grace of immolation, of repentance and of love. Then what does suffering matter? It seems impossible to you? Close your eyes and say with all your soul, 'Jesus, you take care of it'. Do not be afraid, I will take care of things and you will bless my name by humbling yourself. A thousand prayers cannot equal one single act of surrender, remember this well. There is no novena more effective than this:

O Jesus, I surrender myself to You, take care of everything! (Repeat this line 10 times)

Concluding Prayer: Mother, I am yours now and forever. Through you and with you I always want to belong completely to Jesus.

Scripture for Reflection

Realise that God is speaking to you in His Word. Jesus is the Word of God. Ask the Holy Spirit to open your heart so that you may truly hear God speak to you. It is preferable to pray these words aloud, so that they may sink deep within you. And pray them with faith, knowing that God is God and is Lord of all.

*Come to Me, all you who labour
and are overburdened and I will
give you rest.*

Matthew 11:28–30

Fresh and green are the pastures
Where He gives me repose
Near restful waters He leads me
to revive my drooping spirits.

Psalm 22–23:2–3

*Do not be afraid, for I have redeemed you.
I have called you by your name;
you are Mine.*

Isaiah 43:1

You are my hiding place, O Lord;
You save me from distress,
You surround me with cries of deliverance.

Psalm 31–32:7

Commit your life to the Lord,
trust in Him and He will act.

Psalm 36–37:5

*1 am going to lure her and will lead her
out into the wilderness and speak
to her heart.*

Hosea 2:14

She, the faithful one,
whose mind is steadfast,
who keeps the peace,
because she trusts in you.

Isaiah 26:2–3

*W*e know that by turning everything to their good,
God co-operates with all those who love Him, with all
those that He has called according to His purpose.

Romans 8:28

*S*ufferings bring patience, as we know,
and patience brings perseverance,
and perseverance brings hope,
and this hope is not deceptive,
because the love of God
has been poured into our hearts by the
Holy Spirit which has been given us.

Romans 5:3–5

I have loved You with an everlasting love, so I am constant in my affection for You.

Jeremiah 31:3

When you seek Me you shall find Me, when you seek Me with all your heart. I will let you find Me.

Jeremiah 29:13–14

Courage, get up; He is calling you.

Mark 10:50

Peace I bequeath to you,
My own peace I give you,
a peace the world cannot give,
this is My gift to you.
Do not let your hearts be troubled or afraid.

John 14:27

*1 shall give you a new heart and put
a new spirit in you.*

Ezekiel 36:26

*My grace is enough for you:
My power is at its best in weakness.*

2 Corinthians 12:9

*F*ill your minds with everything that is true,
everything that is noble,
everything that is good and pure, everything that we
love and honour,
and everything that can be thought
virtuous or worthy of praise.
Then the God of peace will be with you.

Philippians 4:8–9

1 know the plans I have in mind for you –
it is Yahweh who speaks –
plans for peace, not disaster,
reserving a future full of hope for you.

Jeremiah 29:11, 13

Jesus said, 'I have come so that they may have life and have it to the full.'

John 10:10

*At night there are tears,
but joy comes with dawn.*

Psalm 29–30:5

*C*ast your burden on the Lord and
He will sustain you.

Psalm 54–55:22

If anyone wants to be a follower of Mine,
let him renounce himself and take up his
cross and follow Me.

Matthew 16:24

'Lord, how often should I forgive my brother if he wrongs me? As often as seven times?' Jesus answered, 'Not seven, I tell you, but seventy-seven times.'

Matthew 18:21–22

*1 am the good shepherd; I know My own
and My own know Me.*

John 10:14

*If your lips confess that Jesus is Lord, and if
you believe in your heart that God raised
Him from the dead,
then you will be saved.*

Romans 10:9

*S*ince he clings to me in love, I will free
him, protect him for he knows My name.
When he calls I shall answer:
'I am with you.' I will save him in
distress and give him glory.

Psalm 90–91:14–15

In God alone is my soul at rest.

Psalm 62–63:1

An Extract from Psalm 138–139

O Lord, You search me and You know me,
You know my resting and my rising,
You discern my purpose from afar.
You mark when I walk or lie down,
all my ways lie open to You.
Before ever a word is on my tongue
You know it, O Lord, through and through.
Behind and before You besiege me,
Your hand ever laid upon me.
Too wonderful for me this knowledge,
too high, beyond my reach.
O where can I go from Your spirit,
or where can I flee from Your face?
If I climb the heavens, You are there.
If I lie in the grave, You are there.
If I take the wings of the dawn
and dwell at the sea's farthest end,
even there Your hand would lead me,
Your right hand would hold me fast.
If I say: 'Let the darkness hide me
and the light around me be night',
even darkness is not dark for You
and the night is as clear as the day.

For it was You who created my being,
knit me together in my mother's womb.
I thank You for the wonder of my being,
for the wonders of all Your creation.
Already You knew my soul,
my body held no secret from You
when I was being fashioned in secret
and moulded in the depths of the earth.
Your eyes saw all my actions,
they were all of them written in Your book;
every one of my days was decreed
before one of them came into being.

To me, how mysterious Your thoughts,
the sum of them not to be numbered!
If I count them, they are more than the sand;
to finish, I must be eternal, like You.
O search me, God, and know my heart.
O test me and know my thoughts.
See that I follow not the wrong path
and lead me in the path of life eternal.

Reflections on the Rosary
by St John Paul II

'The Rosary', precisely because it starts with Mary's own experience, is an exquisitely contemplative prayer. Without this contemplative dimension, it would lose its meaning, as St Paul VI clearly pointed out:

Without contemplation, the Rosary is a body without a soul, and its recitation runs the risk of becoming a mechanical repetition of formulas, in violation of the admonition of Christ: 'In praying do not heap up empty phrases as the Gentiles do; for they think they will be heard for their many words' (Matthew 6:7). By its nature the recitation of the Rosary calls for a quiet rhythm and a lingering pace, helping the individual to meditate on the mysteries of the Lord's life as seen through the eyes of her who was closest to the Lord. In this way, the unfathomable riches of these mysteries are disclosed.

It is worth pausing to consider this profound insight of St Paul VI, in order to bring out certain aspects of the Rosary which show that it is really a form of Christocentric contemplation (RVM 14).

With regard to praying for peace and for our families, St John Paul II has the following to say:

As a prayer for peace, the Rosary is also, and always has been, a prayer of and for the family – the family that prays together stays together.

The Holy Rosary, by age-old tradition, has shown itself particularly effective as a prayer that brings the family together. Individual family members, in turning their eyes towards Jesus, also regain the ability to look one another in the eye, to communicate, to show solidarity, to forgive one another and to see their covenant of love renewed in the Spirit of God.

Many of the problems facing contemporary families, especially in economically developed societies, result from their increasing difficulty in communicating. Families seldom manage to come together, and the rare occasions when they do are often taken up with watching television. To return to the recitation of the family Rosary means filling daily life with very different images, images of the mystery of salvation: the image of the Redeemer, the image of His most Blessed Mother. The family that recites the Rosary together reproduces something of the

atmosphere of the household of Nazareth: its members place Jesus at the centre, they share His joys and sorrows, they place their needs and their plans in His hands, they draw from Him the hope and the strength to go on.
(RVM 41).

On Healing

A reflection on healing by
Bishop Martin Drennan, former Bishop of Galway

Seeing their faith, Jesus said to the paralytic, 'My child, your sins are forgiven.' He continued, 'I order you: get up, pick up your stretcher and go off home.' And the man got up, picked up his stretcher at once and walked out in front of everyone (Mark 2:1–12).

❧❧

When we come to meet God in prayer, our hope is that we will return home changed, transformed, by that meeting. This gospel passage invites us to pause and consider that process of transformation in the setting of the Sunday Eucharist. Four elements are singled out – in faith, we come to the Lord's presence, we hear His Word that forgives, we hear His Word that heals our paralysis, we return home saying that God is great.

❧❧

When we come to the Lord, we carry people in our hearts. Like the four men who are mentioned in

this gospel passage, we carry people into the Lord's Presence in faith and let Him surprise them with His Words of forgiveness and healing. Others carry us into God's presence to ask His blessings on us. He speaks His Words of forgiveness so that we may be less unworthy in His presence. What happens is put strongly by the prophet Isaiah, 'I, I am He who blots out your transgressions for My own sake, and I will not remember your sins' (Isaiah 43:25). We may find it difficult to forget our sins, others may remember them, but God forgets them. So, we don't need to carry the past with shame or guilt. In His mercy, God releases us from what makes us immobile.

෧෧

His Word heals our paralysis. For that healing to be effective, we need to name accurately what is paralysing us. Normally, hidden diseases are not cured. The disease that is named may require great skills in those seeking to cure it, but there is no effective way of dealing with what isn't named. When 'hurt' is properly named as 'anger', it is actually easier to look at how to deal with it. There are many pain points that paralyse – unhealed relationships, mistakes, jealousy, envy, greed, prejudice, cynicism, shame, guilt, anxiety and fear. God asks that we be present to Him now. However, we can get stuck in events or memories from the past that caused pain. If pain from the past is not

transformed, then we pass it on. Jesus wants to touch our pain points and heal them. Words have the power to console and bring peace. His Word is always good news, a word that guides us into the way of peace.

Those who witnessed the cure of the paralytic were astonished. They knew that God was the source of the miracle and directed their praise to Him. The aim of the Sunday Eucharist is to send us home saying that God is great. The choir may have been magnificent and maybe the preacher too, but it is to God first and foremost that our praise is to be given. He has done so much for us, given so much, constantly cares so much, that the only fitting response is thanksgiving, wonder at His goodness.

For Prayer on Healing

*Is the word of God helping me to identify
the areas of paralysis in my life?*

৵৶

*If my prayer for healing is not effective,
it might be because it is too vague, not precise
enough in naming what I desire from the Lord.*

৵৶

*Is the Eucharist gradually forming me
into a person of thanksgiving?*

৵৶

Sources and Abbreviations

The authors and publisher would like to thank the following for permission to reproduce text and quotations:

'The Surrender Prayer' is reproduced with permission from The Fr Walter Ciszek Prayer League, Inc., 231 North Jardin Street, Shenandoah, PA 17976, USA.

Extract from Silvester O'Flynn OFM Cap, *The Good News of Mark's Year*. (Dublin: Columba Press, 1990).

Extract from Fr Walter Ciszek, *He Leadeth Me* (New York, Doubleday, 1973).

All quotations from the Psalms are taken from the Grail version, which is used in the Divine Office.
All other scripture quotations are taken from the Jerusalem Bible.

Quotations from St Francis are taken from Regis J. Armstrong, *Francis of Assisi: Early Documents – The Saint* (New York: New City Press, 1999).

Quotations from St Clare are taken from Regis J. Armstrong, *St Clare of Assisi: Early Documents – The Lady* (New York: New City Press, 2006).

Every effort has been made to contact the copyright holders. We apologise for any mistakes or omissions and should any arise we will endeavour to rectify at the earliest possible opportunity.

Other Sources

Extract from the letter of St Thomas More to his Daughter, *The Divine Office Volume III*, © 1974, the hierarchies of Australia, England and Wales, Ireland. (London: Collins, 1974).

Extract from the Diary of St Faustina, *Divine Mercy in my Soul* (Massachusetts: Marians of the Immaculate Conception, 1996).

Pope Francis, *Laudato Si* (2015).

The quotation from St Faustina is from St M. Faustina Kowalska, *Divine Mercy in My Soul* (Massachusetts: Marian of the Immaculate Conception, 1996).

CCC Catechism of the Catholic Church

RVM Rosarium Virginis Mariae

1 LAg First letter to St Agnes of Prague

2 LAg Second letter to St Agnes of Prague

3 LAg Third letter to St Agnes of Prague

4 LAg Fourth letter to St Agnes of Prague

Bl C Blessing of St Clare

PC Acts of the Process of Canonisation of St Clare

L Cl Legend of St Clare

Lt Ord A letter to the Entire Order

Ct Exh Canticle of Exhortation for the Ladies of San Damiano

Acknowledgements

For the immediate help that we have had in putting this book together, we want to thank especially our editor Ciara Doorley, who has been so helpful during this process. We also wish to thank Joanna Smyth and everyone at Hachette Ireland and Noel Cassidy, the graphic designer, who has done a great job and everyone else who has helped us bring this book to fruition.

We have been deeply conscious of how we have been supported in so many ways in writing this book. As we live on Divine Providence, we are constantly in a position of expressing gratitude. The reality of our life is that we would not be here if we were not supported by the people of Galway, primarily, but also by a much wider extended family.

For this we are extremely grateful to those who help us in big ways as well as small. We hope that the book is a fruit of our way of life here and so we dedicate it to all those, known and unknown, who have always been there for us. This book is for you.

The Poor Clares
Nuns' Island
Galway
Ireland